Why You Should ~~Not~~ Pay Your Tithe

Why You Should ~~Not~~ Pay Your Tithe

What Your Pastor May Never Tell You

About Tithes and Offering

VICTOR ANSOR

VICTOR ANSOR PUBLISHING

WHY YOU SHOULD ~~NOT~~ PAY YOUR TITHE

Copyright © 2022 Victor Ansor. All Rights Reserved.

No rights claimed for public domain material, all rights reserved. No parts of this publication may be reproduced, stored in any retrieval system, or transmitted in any form or by any means, electronic, mechanical, recording, or otherwise, without the prior written permission of the author. Violations may be subject to civil or criminal penalties.

Library of Congress Control Number:

ISBN: 978-1-7349631-3-7 (paperback)
ISBN: 978-1-7349631-4-4 (eBook)

Cover Design by Victor Ansor and Emem Ansor

VICTOR ANSOR PUBLISHING

22901 Linden Blvd
PO Box 110423
Cambria Heights NY 11411

Email: victoransorpublishing@yahoo.com
website: victoransor.com

Printed in the United States of America

Also, by the Author

The Spirit of Servanthood

*How to Be Ten Times
Better than Your Peers*

War in The Heavens

Global Holocaust

A Letter to My Late Mom

Table of Contents

DEDICATION xi

THE MANDATE xiii

ACKNOWLEDGMENT xv

APPRECIATION xvii

ANCHOR SCRIPTURE xxi

INTRODUCTION 23

CHAPTER 1: WHAT IS TITHE 29

CHAPTER 2: TITHE IS A PRECIOUS SEED .. 33

CHAPTER 3: TITHE IS HOLY 37

CHAPTER 4: TITHE IS HONOR 41

CHAPTER 5: HOW TO TITHE 45

CHAPTER 6: WHERE TO TITHE 63

CHAPTER 7: THE COVENANT OF TITHING 75

CHAPTER 8: TITHE IS A SPIRITUAL TRANSACTION 81

CHAPTER 9: CORPORATE TITHE 91

CHAPTER 10: TITHE AND OFFERING 95

CHAPTER 11: TITHE AND FIRSTFRUITS ...103

CHAPTER 12: TITHE AND SACRIFICE 109

CHAPTER 13: TITHE AND TAX 115

CHAPTER 14: BENEFITS OF TITHING 121

CHAPTER 15: WINDOWS OF HEAVEN 129

CHAPTER 16: ANALYZING MALACHI 3:10-11 133

CHAPTER 17: HOW TO ENFORCE ANSWERS TO DELAYED RETURNS 141

CHAPTER 18: DO NOT ROB GOD 149

CHAPTER 19: DYNAMICS OF GOD'S KINGDOM FINANCES 153

CHAPTER 20: WHAT GAMBLERS SHOULD KNOW 167

EPILOGUE 173

DEDICATION

To the loving memory of my mother

Agatha who taught me tithing.

THE MANDATE

*Unto me, who am less than the least
of all saints, is this grace given, that
I should preach among the Gentiles
the unsearchable riches of Christ; And
to make all men see what is the fellowship
of the mystery, which from the
beginning of the world had been hid
in God, who created all things by Jesus
Christ: To the intent that now unto the
principalities and powers in heavenly
places might be known by the church
the manifold wisdom of God, According
to the eternal purpose which he
purposed in Christ Jesus our Lord
Ephesians 3:8-11*

ACKNOWLEDGMENT

I acknowledge the almighty God, my Father in heaven, for granting me life. Without Him, I could do nothing. I also acknowledge the person of the Holy Spirit who is my faithful companion. Wisdom and understanding I have none and without the help of the Holy Spirit, I would not be able to write this or any other book. I always sit back to read what I have written and every time I wonder how I did it. To me, that means I am not the one who wrote it, instead it was the Holy Spirit who wrote through me.

This book and all my books have impacted my life and I hope they impact the lives of my readers. By the grace of God, I am just a pen of a ready writer, and I count it a great privilege to be in the service of God and to be an instrument He uses to propagate His Word.

I am thankful to my mother Mrs. Agatha, who has gone to be with the Lord. May her soul continue to rest in the Lord until we meet again when the trumpet sounds. She was instrumental to my being in Christ today. She taught me how to tithe.

Finally, I want to thank you, my readers. Without you, there would be no book. I also want to thank everyone who has encouraged me in one way or the other. May God bless you abundantly.

APPRECIATION

I want to thank all my readers and those who encourage me to keep writing. I want to thank you all for your support and words of encouragement. I want to thank all my friends and those who were instrumental to the successful completion of this book.

Finally, I want to thank those who are unwavering in their prayer adventure for my life and ministry. You are the reason why I am still standing today. May you be greatly rewarded. God bless you.

For Agatha

ANCHOR SCRIPTURE

Malachi 3:10-11

Bring ye all the tithes into the store-house, that there may be meat in mine house, and prove me now herewith, saith the LORD of hosts, if I will not open you the windows of heaven, and pour you out a blessing, that there shall not be room enough to receive it. And I will rebuke the devourer for your sakes, and he shall not destroy the fruits of your ground; neither shall your vine cast her fruit before the time in the field, saith the LORD of hosts.

INTRODUCTION

The subject of tithe has been and is still a controversial issue in the church today. Many do not believe that tithe is part of our duty as Christians, and they don't believe also that it is a scriptural basis for financial prosperity. For many years, Christianity was seen to be a religion of poverty, lack, and want. A call to ministry was a call to pity and ministers of God (pastors) were beggars personified. It was easy to identify a 'pastor' because of his looks. This leaves me to wonder if the old-time believers did not read Zachariah 1:17

> *Cry yet, saying, Thus saith the LORD of hosts;* ***My cities through prosperity*** *shall yet be spread abroad; and the LORD shall yet comfort Zion, and shall yet choose Jerusalem. (KJV)*

WHY YOU SHOULD ~~NOT~~ PAY YOUR TITHE

Christianity is a call to wealth and not poverty but many did not know this and so they made Christian ministry synonymous with poverty. This caused people to run away from Christ and the church. If God will spread his word through prosperity, then the carriers of the message must first be prosperous to spread the gospel. You cannot give what you don't have. **You cannot go telling people God is good without you looking good yourself.** To be prosperous, you must engage in a mystery that will make you prosperous and the mystery is the subject of this book.

In the book of revelation 5:12, the scripture mentions that Jesus died to receive for us riches among other things,

> *Saying with a loud voice, Worthy is the Lamb that was slain to receive power, and **riches**, and wisdom, and strength, and honour, and glory, and blessing. (KJV)*

If Jesus died to receive for us riches, then poverty is against the scripture. To be rich is godly and a good thing that pleases God. If

Jesus receives something for us, then we must accept it and manifest it. When you are poor, it means that you are not walking in the plan and purposes of God for your life. It also means that you are not fulfilling scripture. The bible says in 3 John 2 that it is the will of God for His children to prosper physically and spiritually. *"Beloved, I pray that in every way you may succeed and prosper and be in good health [physically], just as [I know] your soul prospers [spiritually]." (AMP)*. A born-again believer in Christ is expected to be successful, and prosperous in every area of life. Being poor is not humility or holiness and does not glorify God. Paying your tithe is the surest way that will make you rich and being rich is good and scriptural.

Many people argue that tithe is an Old Testament phenomenon, in fact, many have condemned tithe collection by churches insinuating that ministers of God are preying on members to enrich themselves through this medium. This could be true, as some ministers have abused the privilege of their office but that does not make tithing wrong. A young man in my church once told me that he does not believe in tithe, rather he believes in giving his money to the poor instead of paying tithe to the church. What ignorance. According to the scriptures, Abraham paid tithe to Melchisedec when he returned from war. This means that tithing started before the law.

> *For this Melchisedec, King of Salem, priest of the Most High God, who met Abraham returning from the slaughter of the kings, and blessed him; To whom also Abraham gave a tenth part of all; first being by interpretation king of righteousness, and after that also King of Salem, which is, King of peace.*
> *Hebrew 7:1-2 (KJV)*

If we do not believe in tithing or say that tithe is an Old Testament phenomenon, why do we invoke the blessings of Abraham today? Why do we still claim the promises of God in the Old Testament today? Apart from the fact that Abraham paid tithe, the bible still says that Levi, Abraham's son who was not born at the time, paid tithe also through Abraham (you can see more of this in "tithe is a spiritual transaction"). To further prove that tithe is not only an Old Testament phenomenon but also the New Testament phenomenon, Jesus validated tithing in Mathew 23:23

Woe unto you, scribes and Pharisees, hypocrites! For ye pay tithe of mint and anise and cummin, and have omitted the weightier matters of the law, judgment, mercy, and faith: ***these ought ye to have done, and not to leave the other undone.*** *(KJV)*

There has been recorded evidence of enormous benefits of tithing. I am living proof that tithe truly brings prosperity and opens the windows of heaven over men. When you walk under open heavens, you achieve things without struggles, and what others are struggling to get, you just get them without stress. It may not happen immediately, but when your cloud is full, your rain will surely fall Ecclesiastes 11:3. I cannot tell anyone anything that I have not experienced myself. If tithing was not true, I will know because I am an addicted tither, and my life is living proof that

God's word is true. Although an addicted tither, there were times I stopped tithing not because I did not want to but because I was putting so much on my income, and I did not remove my tithe immediately. This made me inconsistent, paying only after a long time. I suffered the consequence and realized that my action was the cause of my problem.

Brethren, the return from tithe far outweighs every argument against it. I have seen lives transformed and ministries, careers, and businesses experience explosive breakthroughs, and many have entered realms of stupendous wealth just by obeying God's word in Malachi 3:10. Therefore, if anything has produced a result and proved to be true, then there is no sense in arguing and fighting or trying to stop it. You only need to try it as God says, "prove me now." We only need to prove God and see if his word is true and not to condemn it.

In this book with the help of the Holy Spirit, I will show you the mystery of tithing in a way you may never have known, and after reading this book and you begin to practice what you learn here; your life will never be the same.

CHAPTER 1

WHAT IS TITHE

Psalm 82:5
They know not, neither will they understand;
they walk on in darkness: all the foundations
of the earth are out of course. (KJV)

The tithe is a spiritual dealing that commits God to release His blessing upon you. It is the kingdom tax that must be remitted.

Many people in the body of Christ do not know what tithe is. A lack of understanding of a thing will make you disregard that thing. The word of God above says, they know not so they continue to walk in ignorance. Lack of knowledge or understanding of a thing makes you walk in the darkness of ignorance concerning that thing. The lack of knowledge or understanding of tithing is the reason many believers are walking in the darkness of poverty and demonic operations.

The reason why many people do not tithe, or tithe wrongly is that they don't know what tithe is. The Merriam Webster online dictionary defines tithe as "a tenth part of something paid as a voluntary contribution or as a tax especially for the support of a religious establishment." This definition is a vivid explanation of what tithe means. The tithe is an unavoidable contribution that must be met. I define tithe **as the spiritual demand that brings God into partnership with man for his financial prosperity**. It is also, as commonly known, the ten percent of your income. A tithe is the total amount of your wage or salary in a week or month, depending on where you live on earth and the method of wage payment. The ten percent of your wage is your tithe. **You are to pay the tithe of all your income in a year**, and since you are not paid your entire year income at once, and you don't make all your money in a year at once, therefore you must pay ten percent of each income as you are paid.

The tithe is not any amount of money you decide to give in a church but the ten percent of your total Income. I have seen people in church on several occasions, who open their wallets and bring out some money, put it in envelop, and write tithe on it. When I ask if that is the ten percent of their income, they simply said no but they just chose to give that as tithe. What a waste. A tithe is either ten percent of your entire income or it is not tithe. When you understand what tithe is, you will be able to engage in it properly.

Understand that tithe is not limited to cash. You are to bring all your tithe to God, and that includes both cash and material things. Anything that comes into your hand is an increase therefore it must be tithed. If you are a farmer, your harvest is an increase and must be tithed. You can either sell your crop after dividing it into ten and take the money to the church or you simply take the tenth part of the crop to church and give it as tithe. May the Lord give you understanding.

CHAPTER 2

TITHE IS A PRECIOUS SEED

They who sow in tears shall reap
with joyful singing.
He who goes back and forth weeping, carrying
his bag of seed [for planting], Will indeed
come again with a shout of joy, bringing
his sheaves with him.
Psalm 126:5-6 (AMP)

Apart from the fact that tithe is ten percent of your total income, the tithe is also a precious seed. One Sunday morning, I was on my way to church with my tithe, and that was the only money I had. Since I cannot eat my tithe, I wept silently within me

WHY YOU SHOULD ~~NOT~~ PAY YOUR TITHE

wondering what will happen when I give all the money as tithe with nothing to fall back on. While this was going on in my heart, a voice quietly speaks the above scripture in my heart, and I stopped crying. A few days later, I had a favor that was mind-blowing. A man in New York gave me a brand-new house to live free without paying a dime for five years. The tithe is a precious seed that yields a bountiful harvest.

A farmer who eats his seed will not have what to plant in the next planting season. When you harvest crops, you keep part of the produce as seed to plant. It is only a fool that will eat what is kept as seed for planting. In the same way, your tithe is the seed that must be kept for planting, and when you eat it, you will not have what to plant and when you don't plant you will not reap. The above scripture says that anyone who has a precious seed and plants it shall certainly return with joy during harvest season. The tithe is a seed that must be planted to have more. Anytime you eat your tithe, you are inviting poverty into your life.

Not paying your tithe is like keeping seed in a jar. Until you remove that seed and plant it on the soil, there will be no fruit. Many believers keep their seed in a jar from year to year while praying to God for open doors. They are not aware that the answer to their prayers is in a jar at home. **Eating your tithe and expecting a financial breakthrough is like asking for a salary where you did not work.** God is a God of principle, and principle is what produces results not prayers. Jesus called principles keys. So, the tithe is a key that unlocks the door of prosperity. If you truly want to be wealthy, use this key (tithe) not prayers and you will be amazed.

Many people in the body of Christ think they can use prayer to bribe God to do something for them while they neglect the principle that is already put in place for their breakthrough. Seed, when not planted, will remain a seed, and no amount of prayer even with forty days of dry fasting can transform a seed. Planting is required for a transformation. Our ignorance as believers will only contribute to suffering, and until we engage the transforming power of principle, our situation and circumstance will remain the same. We are obligated as believers to bring our seed (tithe) into the storehouse of God. When we fail to comply, the economy of the kingdom stays, and heaven closed. Don't eat your seed, plant it.

CHAPTER 3

TITHE IS HOLY

2 Corinthians 6:17
Wherefore come out from among them, and
be ye separate, saith the Lord, and touch not
the unclean thing; and I will receive you. (KJV)

The tithe is holy.

Anything holy must be separated and sanctified for specific use. Tithe must be separated as a holy thing, and whatever is holy must remain untouched. When you spend your tithe, you have committed two offenses, and these are: you rob God, and you eat a holy thing.

WHY YOU SHOULD ~~NOT~~ PAY YOUR TITHE

1. YOU ROB GOD.

When you rob God, you are curse with a curse and when God curse you, no one can lift the curse. Malachi 3:9

2. YOU EAT A HOLY THING.

When a thing is holy and separated to God, you are not to touch it.

It is very clear that many believers do not understand what tithe is, and that is why they do not fulfill this kingdom obligation as they are supposed to. There are so many Christians who want to prosper and are ready to do whatever God ask of them so they can take full delivery of their inheritance but at the same time are ignorant of what is demanded of them. It is so sad that some ministers of the gospel have not taught their members what tithe is except only to shout at the top of their voice that members should bring their tithe, without first taking the time to teach them what tithe is and how to go about it. Now that you know what tithe is, I believe you are beginning to see tithing in a different light.

The tithe is holy. Do not touch your tithe, don't use it to do philanthropy or add to pay your bills. When a thing Is holy, you don't touch it. Using your tithe to pay hospital bill for your parent in the village is a violation of principle. You cannot use your tithe to bless a pastor and expect returns. In fact, giving your tithe to a man of God as a gift result in you robing God, and losing that money. It is better to pay your tithe than to give a prophet offering because the former is a command and a principle while the latter is convenience.

Your tithe is holy and when paid, makes your remaining income secure. It will surprise you to know that as soon as you pay your tithe, God releases His angel to begin to organize favor for you. The remaining money will supernaturally be enough, and you will live within your means. The devil knows this and tries everything to stop you from engaging it. He whispers to you that you have a lot to do with money but then help you spend the money on worthless things that you don't need. Some things you spend money to buy are not

WHY YOU SHOULD ~~NOT~~ PAY YOUR TITHE

necessary and when you pay your tithe, God will help you to use your money judiciously.

The tithe is holy and must be treated so. When you collect your wage, remove the tithe immediately to avoid contamination. With the development of online giving platform, you can send your tithe as soon as you are paid to avoid delay. Treating tithe as a holy thing will help you to be prompt in your payment and release the blessing of God upon your life.

CHAPTER 4

TITHE IS HONOR

Proverb 3:9
Honour the Lord with thy substance….. (KJV)

When you pay your tithe, you are honoring the Lord.

A born-again Christian who brings his or her tithe to God is showing honor and respect to God. Our tithe indicates that we acknowledge God to be absolute and the authority that we submit to. Tithing is more than remitting ten percent of our income. It shows that we acknowledge the supremacy of God over our lives and that He owns everything that we have. It is a form of submission to God. The job that we go to or business that we do belongs to God. It is not our effort, intelligence or ability that gives us what we have but the Divine God who gives us everything richly to enjoy 1 Timothy 6:17

Charge them that are rich in this world, that they be not highminded, nor trust in uncertain riches, **but in the living God, who giveth us richly all things to enjoy. (KJV)**

It is God that owns all that we have. 1 Corinthians 4:7 says "for who makes you different from anyone else? **What do you have that you did not receive?** And if you did receive it, why do you boast as though you did not?" Anything we ever acquire in life is given to us and the knowledge of this would make us release anything that God demands from us freely. When we bring our tithe to God, we are also worshiping God in the process. It is a surrendering of ourselves and finances to God.

It would be interesting to know that not many born again, Holy Spirit filled Christians surrender their finances to God. I believe the greatest worship is when we surrender our finances to God on the altar of tithes, offering and sacrifices. **If God is not Lord over your**

finances, then He is not Lord over you. When you worship the Lord with your tithes, He is truly your Lord. When you overcome money by giving then you are a true victor. Money rules many people that is why they come up with every excuse not to give. Giving our tithes shows honor and worship and make God to be Lord over our lives in earnest.

CHAPTER 5

HOW TO TITHE

Hosea 4:6
My people are destroyed for
lack of knowledge.... (KJV)

God does not bless ignorance.

The reason why God answered prophet Elijah by fire was not because of the way he prayed, but the way he presented his sacrifice.

And he put the wood in order, and cut the bullock in pieces, and laid him on the wood, and said, fill four barrels with water, and pour it on the burnt sacrifice, and on the wood.
1Kings 18:33 (KJV)

WHY YOU SHOULD ~~NOT~~ PAY YOUR TITHE

There are ways of doing things in the kingdom of God if you want result. In the story of Cain and Abel, the bible says, Cain and Abel brought sacrifice to God, but God had respect, meaning he received Abel's sacrifice and rejected that of Cain, Genesis 4:4-5. Since we know from the previous chapter that tithe is the ten percent of our income, I will stress here that **tithe is the ten percent of your gross earning and not net.** Gross earning or wage is the total amount of your income before tax and other deductions. While net is the total amount of wage after tax and other deductions.

Your real income is the total amount of your wage before tax and any deduction. That is why you are not happy when your employer deducts too many things from your wage before paying you. Many people pay tithe from their net income instead of their gross and they have been doing this faithfully expecting the blessing and it never came. When you pay your tithe from your net instead of gross, you have no tithe record in heaven. Anytime you pay your tithe wrongly, God transfers it to your offering record. So many people have been giving offering and not tithe. This is the reason such people complains that tithe does not work and so they discourage others from paying.

To tithe properly and effectively, you must pay from your gross, no matter how much has been deducted. Also, do not tie your income to anything that will deduct your money before you are paid. Living a life of debt and paying back as soon as money comes in is the undoing of many. God can bless you in a way that you can afford all that you need when you need them if you are a faithful tither. **Your income is not enough and will never be enough as long as you don't pay your tithe** or tithe wrongly.

As a businessperson or self-employed, your tithe is the total amount of your profit. For example, if you invest a hundred dollars ($100.00) into a business and it yields a hundred and fifty dollars ($150.00) at the end of the business. Your profit in that business is fifty dollars ($50.00) and so you pay ten percent of the fifty dollars as tithe. If you are doing the kind of business where people call you to render service and then pay you, if you bought anything to use in rendering the service, you should deduct the amount of money you used in buying the item and what remains, you pay your tithe from there. You do not deduct tax from your income before paying your tithe. Government tax and every other kind of levy on your income are not expenses. Expenses are the things you bought to do business.

TITHE PROMPTLY

Tithing requires promptness, it must be done as soon as you collect your wage. As soon as you collect your wage, release the tithe, do not keep it, and expect to pay when you like because if you delay, the enemy will bring too many issues of concern your way that will make you touch your tithe. **The promptness of your payment will help you escape the temptation of spending your tithe**. This happened to me, and I learned my lesson the hard way. I delayed in releasing my tithe and it caused me not to tithe for a long time. I kept saying I will calculate my tithe and it run into several months of not tithing. Then I notice that I was not making money the way I used to. I also noticed that some things started happening to me. My car tire started losing air for no reason and I kept adding it till I got tired. Mysteriously, as soon as I paid my tithe that did not happen again. You may say what is air in a tire, well it may sound like nothing to you, but it sure wore me out. When I had to stop by to fill the air every morning in the winter cold that is something. Apart from that, I began to experience loses in my business, instead of progressing, I was going down daily. I had to advice myself. Prompt payment will help you to be consistent in your kingdom demand of tithing.

TITHE PROPERLY

To tithe, you must do it properly. Many people come to church and there remember that they have tithe money in their wallet which they mixed up with other money and so they collect envelop from the usher, bring out the tithe and pay. This is a very wrong way of paying tithe and I have seen many people do this in church on very many occasions, including pastors. When you collect your wage and let's say your wage is a hundred dollars; your tithe of that

WHY YOU SHOULD ~~NOT~~ PAY YOUR TITHE

hundred dollar is ten dollars and so you remove the ten dollars and put it in an envelope, seal it and write tithe on the envelop so you don't forget. Then you pray on that tithe using Malachi 3:10-11, and the next church service, you take it there and drop in the offering basket. When you do this, you don't need any other prayer, just drop your tithe because you have prayed at home.

Many time we Christians take things casually and the way you take God's thing is the same way he will take you. It is not proper for people to see the amount of money you are giving in church. To avoid this, take envelops home to put your tithe for every Sunday service. When an usher gives you envelop in church, people around you will look to see what you are giving. It doesn't matter if you are rich or poor, make your giving private, let it be between you and God. If you are a pastor that run multiple services in your church, prepare your giving at home for all the services. Don't reach out for envelops in front of the members and struggle with money from your wallet to give, it doesn't look good. Be professional. God likes it when we act well in His house, it shows the spirit of excellence.

TITHE IN RIGHTEOUSNESS

Pay your tithe in righteousness. The scripture in Isaiah 61:8 says, *"For I the Lord love judgment, I hate robbery for burnt offering; and I will direct their work in truth, and I will make an everlasting covenant with them."* God wants us to do the right thing and hates evil ways. Stealing from people and paying tithe from the proceeds brings a curse. Don't do prostitution and pay your tithes from it. It is not only when you stand by a hotel every night to be picked up by different men that is prostitution. Sleeping with different men or women that you are not married to is prostitution and paying tithe from the money they give to you is evil. Sleeping with men to bring jobs or contract to your company is prostitution and whatever money they pay you in the process should not find its way to the church.

Many people do dubious things and are not afraid to give God offering from them. Defrauding people to make gain is bad and

WHY YOU SHOULD ~~NOT~~ PAY YOUR TITHE

lying to make sales makes your income unrighteous. God says He will direct your work in truth. If you don't earn money in righteousness, please don't pay your tithe from it. Money collected from sugar daddy or mummy should not be given to God as offering or tithe. Make sure your income is clean before you take it to church, God is judge. Any pastor who collects money from you knowing that you are involved in a dirty business will incur the judgement of God. If he tells you that your money is blessed because you gave him the tithe is a lie from the pit of hell.

The reason why many die untimely, are sick with incurable diseases or plaque with many misfortunes despite being a committed member of a church could be that they bring accursed money into the house of God. "But the children of Israel committed a trespass in the accursed thing: for Achan, the son of Carmi…..took of the accursed thing: and the anger of the Lord was kindled against the children of Israel." Joshua 7:1. When Achan stole and brought the goods to the camp, he brought in a curse and the consequence was devastating. Anytime you bring money that is not clean to the church, you bring evil and return with a curse. Save yourself from destruction, don't give money that you know was ill gotten either as tithe or offering. God does not need it. If you are a pastor, teach your members the consequences of ill-gotten money. It is not every offering that you must receive. Be truthful in your business, let your yes be yes and no, no so that your wage or income can remain clean. Internet and credit card fraud is evil, the money from such should not be given to God. Your boyfriend's money is unrighteous and should not be tithed. If you are living in sin, repent and rededicate your life to Jesus, change your ways, do your business or job in righteousness and your tithe will be acceptable to God.

TITHE WILLINGLY

Give your tithe willingly not coercively. 2 Corinthians 8:12 says *"For if there be first a willing mind, it is accepted according to that a man hath, and not according to that he hath not."* When you bring your offering to God, let it be willingly. Don't give as if you are forced to give. Don't give

WHY YOU SHOULD ~~NOT~~ PAY YOUR TITHE

because the pastor asked you to, or your friend forced you to give. Although tithe is a requirement, it must still come from a willing mind. Let it be something you want to do not what you are compelled to do. God loves it when we are willing to do something for Him, and He always reward a willing mind lavishly. Do not pay your tithe as though you are doing God or the church a favor. God does not need your money, He owns everything. When you did not tithe, the work of God was going on and if you stop tithing, it will continue. Your willingness to pay your tithe to advance the purposes of God on the earth is for your good. God can command resources from anywhere to get things done, He does not depend on you. When you understand this, you will see it as a privilege to give to Him. Do not allow a pastor to force you to give. Any man of God that ask you to pledge a certain amount of money for church project, please ignore him. God cannot force you to give. Don't allow anyone to put unnecessary stress or debt on you. Learn to give what you have and willingly.

TITHE JOYFULLY

Learn to give with a joyful heart. Don't bring your tithe frowning as if you are not happy with God. God loves a cheerful giver. Be joyful with your seed in hand. Psalm 100:2 says, *"Serve the Lord with gladness: come before his presence with singing."* When you carry your tithe to church, be glad and even sing praises acknowledging God as the source. Don't give and complain or murmur.

TITHE RESPECTFULLY

Many Christians are fond of selecting bad and torn bills to give as tithe while they keep the clean bills for themselves. God is a great king, and you cannot give to him what you can't even give to your governor. Malachi 1:13-14

> *Ye said also, Behold, what a weariness is it!*
> *and ye have*
> *snuffed at it, saith the Lord of host;*
> *and* **ye brought what**
> **was torn, and the lame, and the sick;** *thus,*
> *ye brought an offering:*

WHY YOU SHOULD ~~NOT~~ PAY YOUR TITHE

> *should I accept this of your hand?*
> *Saith the Lord. But **cursed***
> ***be the deceiver, which had***
> ***in his flock a male, and voweth,***
> ***and sacrificeth unto the Lord a corrupt thing**:*
> *for I am a great King,*
> *saith the Lord of host, and my name is*
> *dreadful among the heathen. (KJV)*

Giving God bad dollar bills disqualifies your giving. God calls such a person a deceiver and even curse the individual because they choose to give God what is bad and keep the good for themselves. I was fond of doing this a lot growing up. When my mother gave us money to put as offering, if the money is clean, I will keep it and put the bad bills. That was bad although I was a child and I believe God overlooked but it will be a gross offense to continue in such act as an adult.

When you pay your tithe, you have made the remaining to be holy, and it will be enough. Do not let your children school fees make you touch your tithe. If what you have is not enough then touching your tithe will not make it enough either. It will continue not to be enough until you start tithing.

As a housewife, you can tithe from the house keeping money that your husband gives to you. The reason why you must tithe from it is because you are given the money to spend at your discretion. When you tithe from the money, the remaining will be enough for the family upkeep. You may be surprised how you will start getting good deals in the market. Your food stuffs at home may not finish quickly as it used to. Your neighbors may mysteriously start giving you stuffs you never expect. It can even happen that the more you spend the money, the more it increases. God can decide to bless you in a way that food never finish in your house.

My wife is a faithful tither and when we got married something miraculous happened. We received lots of gift items aside from the cash gifts that we had to rent a storage to keep them. Everything that my wife desired came as gifts. Till this moment we have not open many of the gifts. Many things we use in our house came as a gift. This is what God alone can do if you are a faithful tither. When our first child was born

WHY YOU SHOULD ~~NOT~~ PAY YOUR TITHE

the same thing happened; we received so many gifts and until now we have not bought any diaper or wipes for our baby. God can do the same for you.

As a student, you cannot tithe your school fees, but you can tithe your pocket money. No matter the amount of money given to you, you should remove the ten percent of that amount and set it aside and when you get to church you pay.

You should not pay tithe from osusu (contribution) money. If you are in a group of people who contributes money weekly or monthly and each member of that group take turn to pick the money, you don't need to pay tithe when it is your turn to pick the money because you had paid your tithe before paying the osusu.

Tithing is not limited to salary or wages; you should pay tithe from gifts also because anything that comes into your hand is increase. If someone gives you twenty dollars, your tithe from that money is two dollars and you must pay it. If you are given a material gift, you must pay tithe from it. Let's say someone gives you ten bags of rice as gift, the tithe from that gift is one bag of rice and you must take it to church and give. If you don't want to take the bag of rice to church, you can value the bag of rice and pay the cost in cash. If you are given a car as gift, you cannot divide the car into ten, so you value the car and pay ten percent of the cost of the car but if you don't have that to pay, you don't need to worry, for God is not a task master but if you have, pay. The cash gifts you receive during your wedding and baby dedication should be tithed. Anytime money enters your hand for you to spend, the ten percent of that money belongs to God.

Some people are fond of writing a check which include tithe and offering and then give. Let me ask you, how do you expect the church to know that the check you wrote is for tithe and offering and how do you expect them to separate the amounts? Many of us thinks that when we come to church, we can do anything and expect God to understand. There is order in heaven. If you have been writing both your tithes and offering as one amount in a check

WHY YOU SHOULD ~~NOT~~ PAY YOUR TITHE

without any information to distinguish them or to show that it is tithe and offering, then know that it was not recorded in heaven as tithe. **If your church officials were left confused not knowing where to record the money, heaven will not do magic either**. They will push that money to offering and that means all the while you were giving offering thinking you were paying tithe.

Technology has made it easier now for people to give in church. Many churches have switched fully to online giving due to COVID-19 pandemic. This is good because you don't need to go to church before you pay your tithe. As soon as you get money, you can Zelle or use your church online giving platform to give. There are no more excuses for not paying tithe. If you are a pastor, it is important to go fully online in your giving because it will help your church to properly account for every money and make it less stressful for members.

If you have many businesses with money flowing in from many sources, I will advise that you pay an accountant to oversee your tithe to help you pay accurately. Having an accountant for tithing purposes is very needful especially for businesspeople and shows how great God has blessed you.

CHAPTER 6
WHERE TO TITHE

Deuteronomy 12:13
*Take heed to thyself that thou **offer not thy burnt offerings in every place that thou seest: But in the place which the LORD shall choose** in one of thy tribes, there thou shalt offer thy burnt offerings and there thou shalt do all that I command thee. (KJV)*

There is a place to pay your tithe.

It is not every church or individual you see that you pay your tithe to. Before you pay your tithe, you must be a member of a local church then you can pay your tithe there. **Your tithe is for your local church.** For your tithe to

WHY YOU SHOULD ~~NOT~~ PAY YOUR TITHE

be acceptable, you must first give your life to Jesus, accept him as your lord and personal savior, and then belong to a church. The bible says in Malachi 3:10,

Bring ye all the tithe into the store house.

How can you bring your tithe into a store house (church) that you are not a part of? You must be a member of a local church to pay your tithe. You don't walk into any church and give your tithe, no matter how much you give, you have just lost that money because it is not accepted, and it is not recorded to your account in heaven as tithe.

If you have not given your life to Jesus and you have been giving churches or individuals money in the name of paying tithe, this is the opportunity to start doing it right. Please pray this simple prayer after me in the sincerity of your heart and you will be born again.

Lord Jesus, I come to you. I know I am a sinner, and I believe you came and died for me that I might be saved. I accept you Jesus as my Lord and Savior. Thank you, Jesus, for forgiving me. Thank you for

saving me. Now I know my sins are forgiven. I am saved. I am born again. I am a child of God; old things are passed away and behold all things are become new. In Jesus name, Amen.

If you prayed the above prayer sincerely, you are now born again. Look for a bible believing church and establish yourself as a member and start serving God with your tithe. If you have difficulty deciding where to worship, I invite you to look for Living Faith Church Worldwide (aka) Winners Chapel, or Winners Chapel International and there make it your church.

Tithe is for your local church where you are nurtured spiritually. You cannot be an American citizen and be paying your tax to China, likewise you cannot be nurtured spiritually in the Baptist church, and you pay your tithe to Anglican church. Like tax which you are constitutionally obligated to pay to your country, tithe is to be paid to your local church where you are established. This aspect of tithing has been violated by many that is why they don't have returns from their tithes. Remember

WHY YOU SHOULD ~~NOT~~ PAY YOUR TITHE

you **pay** your tithe but **give** your offering. Paying and giving are two different things.

If you are a member of a particular church which has branches, your tithe is for the local branch which you attend always. If for any reason you travel out to somewhere and decide to worship in another branch of that same church, you don't pay your tithe there, instead you give your offering but reserve your tithe for your local branch until you return then you pay. But if you are relocating from where you are to another place, then you can start paying your tithe in the new place if you know that you are not going back to your former place of worship. This applies to relocating to another location and start worshiping in a new church other than the church you were formerly a member.

It is a gross misconduct and spiritual ignorance to send pastors and churches that you don't attend always tithe simply because it is your former church or family church. If you use to attend a church with your family while growing up, and you left to start life or school in another place; the church that you now attend consistently is your store house, that is where your tithe belongs. I have seen people send their tithe to their village church that they visit once a year instead of the one they are attending every week. It is better not to pay your tithe than to send it to where you are not nurtured spiritually.

Please understand that your local church is responsible for your spiritual wellbeing. They pray for you and releases blessing upon you every time they gather which you always shout a big amen. It is wrong for you to take the money that is supposed to pay the pastor's salary and run the church to go and give another who does nothing for you.

Some people have men of God in different locations where they send their tithes so they can pray for them. Know that **asking people to pray for you and you compensating them with your tithe is wrong and stupid**. The little prayer your local pastor prays for you goes a long way and is answered in heaven. Any place you pay for prayer is a waste because the prayer is not answered. God is divine and a God of knowledge.

WHY YOU SHOULD ~~NOT~~ PAY YOUR TITHE

As a pastor, if you go to minister in another church and you are given a gift of money, you should remove your tithe from that money to pay as tithe when you return to your local church. Giving tithes to pastors as gift is wrong and a waste. You can only give a pastor what is called "prophets offering" but not your tithe. Pastors who collect tithes personally from members and start spending them are committing serious error. Tithe is not for pastors personal spending; it is for the store house. Those pastors who are sole administrator of their church, they handle everything so that no one will touch the money in the church as if the money belongs to them are only doing so out of ignorance, greed, and foolishness. Even though you are the founder of your church, that church does not belong to you, Jesus says in Mathew 16:18

> *And I say also unto thee, That thou art Peter, and upon this rock **I will build my church;** and the gates of hell shall not prevail against it. (KJV)*

The church is Jesus's and every money that comes into his church must be properly accounted for. No matter how small your church might be, get people to handle the money. **As a pastor, stay away from church money** if you want to succeed. I believe that integrity builds and prosper a ministry more than anything else because if you pray all the prayer and lack integrity by using church money for your gain, that ministry will fall, prayer notwithstanding. When someone comes to pay tithe, refer them to the office where the money will be collected and properly documented; in doing so, you have not only proven yourself to be a man of integrity, but have brought the blessing of God upon the church you are pastoring.

I used to walk into any church I see and drop my tithe in the tithe box and sometimes I will just keep it on the alter and left thinking that God has received it. I was tithing but I was doing it wrongly and so the blessing did not come, and my business was going down by the day until I went bankrupt even-though my tithes were in dollars and very bulky. I believe

WHY YOU SHOULD ~~NOT~~ PAY YOUR TITHE

that God saw my heart that I love to give and so he redirected my ways and brought me to knowledge so I can do it properly and ever since I have been blessed beyond measure.

There were times I use to pay large amount of money as tithe to priests and pastors who were my friends, yet I was not blessed. So not paying at the right place is like not paying at all. Everyone has a pastor assign to them by God and a church they must serve God through, and you must locate your pastor and your local church and serve God there with your tithe and you will see good things begin to happen in your life.

> *Jeremiah 3:15*
> *And I will give you pastors according*
> *to mine heart, which shall feed you*
> *with knowledge and understanding. (KJV)*

You have been given a pastor to feed you spiritually and in return you bring your tithe to the store house where that pastor is so that it can be used to make things work in that particular house. Your tithe is what is used in building that church or pay the rent as the case may be. It is used in paying the pastor and workers salary or wage. It is used also to pay the light and gas bill. The communion you take, and all the things required to run the church comes from your tithe just like what the government uses your tax to do in providing basic amenities for your everyday use. The larger the church, the bigger the financial demand. This means that if you don't pay your tithe, the church may not be able to function properly for lack of financial resources.

Every organization needs money to run daily operation. **You cannot dress cute and come to church every Sunday without giving what is needed to run that church.** Some may ask, what about offering? My answer is, how much do you give as offering? You cannot compare tithe to offering. **Tithe is a demand while offering is a freewill**, and since offering is a freewill, find out how much people give in a year, and you will be amazed. Your one dollar in an envelope every Sunday cannot run the church. Your tithe which come from your income could be substantial collectively.

WHY YOU SHOULD ~~NOT~~ PAY YOUR TITHE

Remember, it is the pastor that you called for prayers when your child is sick, or your husband is sacked from work. When you buy a new car, it is your pastor that you call to dedicate. **Where do you think the money for the anointing oil used in dedicating your car comes from?** Your pastor conducts your wedding and name your child, so it is proper to pay your tithe to your local assembly where you are blessed with all these services.

Many church members don't allow their pastors to rest, even at midnight they call him for prayers just because someone pursued them in the dream. They even call the pastor to settle marital problems but to pay their tithe, they complain. **Your tithe is a demand and until you pay, you are in debt to heaven.**

Many have accused pastors of eating tithes and some even accuse wealthy men of God of using their tithes to buy private jet. I am not a pastor, and I don't own any church where I collect tithes and offering; I write this by the inspiration of the Holy Spirit. Any ministry or pastor that owns private jet, uses such to propagate the gospel. Many pastors have great anointings that requires them to be in different places around the world to preach. To own a private jet is a great responsibility and you must need it to have one. The cost of maintenance, parking and paying a pilot is enormous. If your pastor has one, that means God has bless your church and the anointing on that pastor is sought after. Your tithe to the church should not make you talk against that church. You cannot castigate your pastor for being rich and still receive blessings from him.

Notwithstanding, if a pastor uses church money to acquire a private jet just to measure up when he doesn't need it, that is his problem with God. Your responsibility is to pay your tithe and not to question how it is used. Your tithe although is used to run the church is for God. Whatever it is used for is none of your business. God will judge whoever misappropriate His finances but your own is to remain obedient. We will get ourselves out of trouble if we stop castigating churches and men of God. God is judge not church members. Our eternal reward is in what we do not what others do. Any church you are planted as a member, pay your tithe there. Be involved in advancing the kingdom in that local church and close your eyes to whatever anyone or pastor does with money. Your tithe is to God not man.

CHAPTER 7

THE COVENANT OF TITHING

Genesis 8:22
While the earth remaineth, seedtime
and harvest.....shall not cease. (KJV)

You can never find anyone who prayed himself into prosperity.

For you to experience the financial fortune that redemption offers every born-again child of God, you must be a tither. The tithe is a covenant, and this covenant is the covenant of seedtime and harvest. According to the covenant, seedtime will always precede harvest time. Your tithe is the seed and when you pay, you have planted a seed that must yield a harvest. God cannot go against the principle which he set in motion. You cannot reap what you did not sow. And God says in Psalm 89:34

> *My covenant will I not break, nor alter the thing that is gone out of my lips. (KJV)*

God cannot break his covenant. If He says that seedtime and harvest shall not cease then all you need to do is sow, for you will certainly reap. There is a covenant between the earth and seed that is why anytime you plant a seed in the ground, it must grow. As I said earlier that tithe is a seed, so when you pay your tithe, the covenant of seedtime and harvest is set in motion that will make you reap what you sowed. God cannot break his covenant therefore your tithe as a seed must germinate, grow and bring a harvest. When you collect your wage and pay your tithe, it means you have planted ten percent of your previous harvest. Every time you collect your wage it is your harvest season and when you plant the seed from the harvest, you are sure of harvest in the next season. This is very spiritual.

Bishop David Oyedepo who is the father of tithe in this age gave an astounding account of how God revealed to him the secret of kingdom prosperity. He said, "I went on three days of fasting and prayers in search of financial prosperity. On the third day the heavens open and God said- "my prosperity plan is not a promise, so it does not answer to prayer, and it has no respect for fasting. My prosperity plan is a covenant and until your part is played, I am not committed." This is the word of God directly from God to a man who went searching for the secret of God's kingdom financial prosperity. God made it clear to his servant that His prosperity plan is a covenant and that no matter how hard you pray and how many days you fast, you can never access His prosperity until you subscribe to the covenant.

Therefore, when you pay your tithes, God is committed to opening the windows of heaven over you. Bishop David Oyedepo is a man I love and respect and, he has impacted my life greatly. He has faithfully engaged in the covenant of tithing and the result is very conspicuous. He is now said to be the richest pastor in the world, yet he does not receive a salary from the church nor receive a royalty from the books he writes. You see, this is what it means for the windows of heaven to open over a man. It can also open for you, no need for envy.

We understand that a covenant is an agreement between two parties and in this case, between God and man. I have never seen any agreement where the other party is begged into fulfilling his part of the agreement. The tithe is a covenant and when you enter this covenant with God, He is faithful and will never disappoint. If you as a mortal, pay your tithe faithfully, why will an invisible and Holy God not keep his own side?

Many Christians prefer to run around looking for who to pray or prophecy to them to prosper when the only thing they are supposed to do is engage in the covenant of seedtime and harvest. Understand that every other giving in the kingdom will certainly bring you returns, but the tithe is the only giving that comes with a guarantee of security.

You can give a big offering, sponsor great church projects, and take care of the needy in your community. These are all good spiritual investments and God will always bless you abundantly, but there is no guarantee of protection from the demonic assault upon those blessings. Imagine a scenario where a farmer finish planting his crops and the harvest come. When he is about to harvest the crops, insects begin to eat the crops, and even after getting some of the harvests to his barns, robbers come and steal them at night. This is what happens to the returns from other giving. But God says that when you pay your tithe, he will not allow devourer to come near you. So, the tithe is the only giving that will give you rest when you engage.

Know that devourers have been released into the world and they are having a field day. When you watch your television, you will understand what is going on around the world. No one is truly safe anymore but security from tithing can hide you from any assault the enemy may release.

WHY YOU SHOULD ~~NOT~~ PAY YOUR TITHE

During the COVID 19 Pandemic, many people died while others spend time in the hospital with little hope of surviving. COVID 19 is a devourer and tithe can stop it from coming to you and your family. I believe that something greater than COVID 19 will come, and your only place of security is to engage a convent that provides security. The tithe is the only giving that guarantees security. I pray that as you read this, you will begin to engage faithfully in tithing so that the covenant will work for you.

CHAPTER 8
TITHE IS A SPIRITUAL TRANSACTION

Hebrew 7:8
And here men that die receive tithes;
but there he receiveth them, of whom
it is witness that he liveth. (KJV)

The tithe is a spiritual transaction between man and a deity.

A transaction is a business conducted by two people, and in this case between God and man. The tithe is a spiritual transaction, and the lack of this understanding makes people either disregard it, take it for granted, or outrightly ignore it. When

WHY YOU SHOULD ~~NOT~~ PAY YOUR TITHE

the value of a thing is not known, abuse is inevitable said, Myles Munroe. When you go to church and give your tithe, you are doing a spiritual transaction. When you pay your tithe at the church office or put your tithe in the offering basket, the ushers will collect it, but Jesus is the one who receives it in heaven. The above scripture says that here men that die receive tithe, but there he receives them, this means that although people you see with your eyes collect tithes from you, the real person you are paying it to is the Lord Jesus who is seated in heaven, and he lives forever. When Jesus was here on the earth, he demonstrated this authority by sitting in the temple and watching what everyone was giving.

> *And Jesus sat over against the treasury, and beheld how the people cast money into the treasury: and many that were rich cast in much.*
> *Mark 12:41 (KJV)*

Now with absolute authority, Jesus sits in heaven and not only to watch how we give but also to receive our giving. Your tithe goes straight into your tithe account in heaven, you may ask, do I have an account in heaven? oh yes, you do.

For even in Thessalonica ye sent once and again, unto my necessity. Not because I desire a gift: but I desire fruit that may abound **to your account***.*
Philippians 4:16-17 (KJV)

As a born-again child of God, the day you gave your life to Jesus, which is called the new birth, an account was open in your name in heaven, and anytime you pay your tithe, it is credited into that account; that is why if you have knowledge of this, you can boldly demand a withdrawal. Those who don't pay their tithe don't have a deposit in heaven that is why no matter how much they acquire on earth even as children of God, the devourer still have access in their lives. This is the reason you see born-again Christians, I mean Holy Spirit-filled, tongue-talking believers in hospital emergency room and prison, and you ask why? Don't get me wrong, some tithers may still be challenged, but their tithe always speaks for them and get them out. If you are a thither and you have a health challenge, a court case, or business

WHY YOU SHOULD ~~NOT~~ PAY YOUR TITHE

breakdown, it is time you stand on the word of God and demand restoration.

When Abraham returned from the slaughter of the kings in Genesis 14:18-20 the bible says that he paid a tithe of all to Melchisedec and to show that it is a spiritual transaction, the bible in Hebrew 7:9-10 confirms this.

> *And as I may so say, Levi also, who recieveth tithes, paid tithes in Abraham. For he was yet in the loins of his father, when Melchisedec met him. (KJV)*

Levi was not born when Abraham paid the tithe of all to Melchisedec, but the bible says that he paid tithe through Abraham. This means that tithe is a spiritual transaction that affects generations unborn.

Let's look at this when a man walks into a shrine, the first thing he is asked by the priest is "what have you brought for the gods" it is believed that anytime you go to visit the gods, you must present an offering. The gods are spirits and spirits don't eat but why do they require something from you? Because anything you present to them in that shrine is a spiritual transaction of which they use to afflict the giver. We must understand that the devil duplicates whatever God does. When you give your tithe, you have engaged in a spiritual transaction between you and a deity called God. You pay here on earth and Jesus receives it in heaven that is why the devourer cannot come near you as he is rebuked for your sake.

Many people have experienced business breakthroughs by tithing and when they stopped the business goes down and you cannot explain why. This means that what they did before (tithing) was more spiritual than physical. Abraham paid tithe and God said that Levi who was not born at the time paid also, this is spiritual.

I always tell people that the church is a very spiritual place. **Any place that has an altar, has spirits dwelling there whether anyone is there or not**. The altar in a church is a good altar and it attracts good spirits. God is a deity that is worshiped in a church alter therefore anything you give in that alter is a spiritual transaction between you and the spirit at work in that alter.

That is why people must be careful where they walk into. When Abraham was about to offer Isaac to God as sacrifice and the angel stopped him. Although he didn't kill Isaac, the bible says that God received Isaac in a figure; that means it was a spiritual transaction.

> *Hebrew. 11:19*
> *Accounting that God was able to raise him up, even from the dead; from whence also* **he received him in a figure**. *(KJV)*

When Noah raised an altar and offered sacrifice unto God after the flood, God received it in heaven and change his mind about destroying man again through the flood. Genesis 8:22. That means what Noah did was a spiritual transaction. He reared an alter here on the earth, offered animals as an offering and God smelt it in heaven. Our tithe is a spiritual transaction and when we know it and treat it as such, we will engage in it properly and attract the Father of spirits into our affairs.

Let me use this opportunity to let you know that whatever you do in this life has spiritual implications and eternal consequences. If your life is kingdom focus you will have an eternal reward. The reason why many people do not respond to kingdom demand is that their heart is on this earth, and they don't think eternity. Real-life starts after death. The moment you close your eyes here in this world, you will be amazed at the reality of life after death. As born-again child of God, your home is in heaven and your kingdom investments on this earth accumulate for you there. When you give here, you are making deposits.

Jesus made a profound statement in Mathew 6:19, *"lay not up for yourselves treasures upon earth, where moth and rust doth corrupt, and where thieves break through and steal."* Here Jesus was opening our eyes to the reality of the afterlife. Laying up for ourselves treasures on earth means acquiring things only for this life but no treasures for the afterlife. Paying your tithes and giving for the work of God is a spiritual transaction that accumulates for you in heaven. Please understand that your giving on this earth is not measured by heaven according to size or volume but according to the quality of the heart, motive, and obedience. Tithing is obedience and increases your savings in heaven.

Anytime you obey God and pay your tithe, it deposits something of worth for you in the afterlife, that deposit is not money but something more valuable. When you get this revelation, tithing and other kingdom investments will not be difficult for you. The only thing we carry to the other side of life is not our cars, mansions, or money in the bank but what we do to advance the kingdom of God on the earth.

Spiritual investment is more important than earthly accumulation. It is your work that follows you when you depart this life and not your wealth. Revelation 14:13 says, *"And I heard a voice from heaven saying unto me, Write, Blessed are the dead which die in the Lord from henceforth: Yea, saith the Spirit, that they may rest from their labours; **and their works do follow them.**"* Your tithes will follow you just like other good things you do in life. Your prayers for the kingdoms, souls you win and lives that you touched here build up unimaginable wealth for you in heaven.

Now that you learn this, live a kingdom-conscious life, engage in this spiritual transaction by consistently paying your tithes and your work will follow you.

CHAPTER 9

CORPORATE TITHE

Hebrew 7:9-10
And as I may so say, Levi also, who
recieveth tithes, paid tithes in Abraham.
For he was yet in the loins of his father,
when Melchisedec met him. (KJV)

As believers, the way we pay tithe as an individual, we must also pay as an organization or corporation if we want it to succeed. You can be a tither as an individual but if your business or company does not pay tithe, you will be more successful than your business. If it is only your business that pays you and you are more successful than that business, then you can understand how that will end. The way God blesses individuals who pay tithe is the same way he blesses businesses that pay tithe. The same way God opens the windows of heaven over individual who pays tithe is the same way he opens the windows of heaven over businesses, corporations, and establishments that pays tithe according to Bishop Oyedepo.

Corporate tithing is what every organization must engage in if you want that business to succeed. As a corporate entity, you are to pay the tithe of your income in a year. Since you balance your financial records every month and make payments to management and staff of that organization, your tithe must first be deducted before any expenditure. This also includes church organization. Every church must pay their tithe if they want to succeed financially. The reason why many churches are deep in debt and riddle with court cases is that they have neglected or are ignorant of this kingdom's demand. You will ask, where does or who should a church pay their tithe to? I want to believe that every church has another church ministry where they are spiritually connected to and if they don't, they should look for one.

When a church finds a ministry, they can connect spiritually, they should pay their tithe to that ministry faithfully so that the windows of heaven can be open to that church. I know this will sound ridiculous to many but that is the truth. No matter how much your church income is in a month, you must pay the tithe of all, not to an individual but to another church. Don't say we are using our money to fund humanitarian services, no- tithe is tithe.

As a business owner, the total income of your business at the end of the month must be tithed. If you pay yourself from your business, you must first remove the ten percent of the entire income of that business at the end of the month or week as the case may be. After, you pay yourself from the business and then remove your own personal tithe from your pay. Someone will say "but that is too much" and I will say but you pay tax from your business and your income. You file tax for yourself and still file for your business but when it comes to the matters of the kingdom that is when we see it as too much.

WHY YOU SHOULD ~~NOT~~ PAY YOUR TITHE

If you are running an NGO, you must pay your tithe because everything donated to that NGO is an increase that must be tithed.

Corporate tithing is essential if you must experience open heaven over your organization or business no matter how large or small it might be.

CHAPTER 10

TITHE AND OFFERING

Psalm 96:8
Give unto the Lord the glory due unto his name:
bring an offering*, and come into his courts.*
Also,
1Chronicles 16:29
Give unto the Lord the glory due unto his name:
bring an offering*, and come before him:*
worship the Lord in the beauty of holiness. (KJV)

An offering is dew and rain that water our seed (tithe).

Do not go to church without carrying an offering except you don't have. An offering is very important in church service. The opening scripture says bring an

WHY YOU SHOULD ~~NOT~~ PAY YOUR TITHE

offering. It is not enough to go and sing praises and dance in church, you must present an offering. **No one ever visited a shrine without an offering to the gods.** If devil worshippers present offering to demonic spirits, why can't we give the living God an offering? Your offering should go alongside your tithe. After all the lifting up of holy hands, dance and sweat and even jump when the preacher charges you up put an offering. The deity is very interested in what you bring for him. **Don't go to collect from God every Sunday without having something to give in return.**

The tithe is a kingdom demand that every child of God is obligated to pay, while the offering is free will. The tithe is a command that must be obeyed while the offering is according to the blessing of God upon your life. It is not proper for a child of God to stay without paying tithe. If we as citizens of our nations don't pay our taxes, it will be difficult for the government to provide basic amenities for our use. It is even a crime in some countries if you don't pay your tax. Some governments take tax seriously and failure to pay can lead to arrest and imprisonment, fines, or confiscation of property. If tax is that serious then tithe is serious. In the United States, the Internal Revenue Service IRS is more powerful than any other agency of the government. They can bring down anyone, hunt, and prosecute anyone when it comes to a tax matter.

Many Christians do not know the difference between tithe and offering and so they often interchange one for another. Many people go to church and choose to give any amount of money they find in their wallet as tithe and put the rest as an offering. When we go to church, we must carry something in our hands as an offering to present to God. If you want to go and see the queen or a king, you must carry a gift to present to them. God is a great king, and He sits king forever, therefore when we go to present ourselves before him, we must carry a gift in our hands as an offering. Deuteronomy 16:16-17 says,

WHY YOU SHOULD ~~NOT~~ PAY YOUR TITHE

> *....and they shall not appear before the Lord empty. Every man shall give as he is able, according to the blessing of the Lord thy God which he hath given thee. (KJV)*

God says that we should not appear before him empty. Therefore, in every worship service, we must bring an offering to present to God according to how he has blessed us. You give an offering according to your capacity not because the pastor forces you to or because your friend writes a check of a thousand and you want to do the same when your capacity is a hundred or fifty. **Never give to impress anyone, give according to your level.** Don't give a big offering in the church because a beautiful lady is sitting by you, and you want to impress her. It is according to the blessing of God upon you.

It is wrong to take part of your tithe money to give as an offering. when you do that, you have spoiled the tithe because you were not supposed to touch it in the first place. The tithe is for your local church where you are nurtured spiritually but you can give your offering anywhere you choose.

When you collect your wage, after removing your tithe it is proper to set aside some money which you will give as an offering. This is according to how much you make in a week or month. I will advise you to put this money in envelop and mark offering. When you do this, you will not need to search your wallet during service for what to give.

Your offering should multiply year after year to indicate how God has lifted you. **If your offering of last year was five dollars, for Christ's sake it should change next year.** You cannot keep giving five dollars every year. That is shameful and wicked. When you keep giving the same amount of money every year, you are saying that God has not promoted you and we all know that is not true. **Your offering should reflect your status.**

As God blesses you, let your offering increase to meet your new level. You can't be wearing expensive clothes and be putting five dollars in the offering basket. Some people are also fond of putting empty envelopes in the offering basket. If you don't have anything to give, God understands and there is nothing to be ashamed of, but you must not deceive yourself by putting an empty envelope in the offering basket. When you do that, you only succeed in taking a curse back home instead of a blessing. God is a great King. Now that churches are going digital in their giving, some people will lift their phones during offering time pretending that they gave. Stop lying to God and yourself, be sincere.

Your offering must be clean and presentable. Don't put torn bills in church, and don't write on the bill before giving. Your money must be put in an envelope and sealed.

Learn to give your children an offering before they leave for church. Don't begin to look for your child or they run around looking for you when it is offering time. As a parent, stop giving your children one dollar as an offering. You spend big in the restaurant and fast food for your children, why not teach them how to give big. I see children running around the church with one-dollar bills to put in the offering basket. Teach your children how to give, and properly. Put their offering in an envelope and let them learn early how to present it to God.

Some church members are fund of going to the bathroom when it is offering time. For goodness' sake, what are you running from? Giving to God brings blessing and not poverty. Those who run away from giving will eventually give lots of money to their girlfriend that same day in fact immediately after service. Some ladies prefer to buy expensive hair and makeup rather than put an offering. If you are not afraid to spend big money on groceries, why are you running away from giving? If you dress expensive to church, you should give big. Your offering should reflect your dance or your looks. You should not dance a thousand-dollar dance and put ten dollars neither should you wear an expensive tie and smuggle five dollars into the offering basket.

When you go to church, have the consciousness that you are going to appear before a great king so let your offering show that you honor and respect Him. The time for an offering is not the time to go to the bathroom or go outside to chat. Even when you don't have money, sit down in the church so that God will see you and change your story. Proverb 11:25

says that *"a generous person will prosper; whoever refreshes others will be refreshed."* (NIV) If you are generous to God with your money, He will make your purse fat. It is very Important to be a giver and when you refresh God's house, He will refresh you more. Giving an offering will make God bless you and everything you do.

CHAPTER 11

TITHE AND FIRSTFRUITS

*Honour the Lord with thy substance, and
with the firstfruits of all thine increase.*
Proverb 3:9 (KJV)

There is a conflict which I observe every time someone has a new job and collects the first salary. Many people are always confused as to what to do with their first wage or salary. A lot of people use their first wage to buy clothes to appear good-looking especially if they had stayed for a long time without a job or just finish college. While others use their first wage to throw a party to celebrate their new job, the rest put the money in the bank wondering what to do with it. Born again Christians are not exempted from this error as some of them remove their tithe and then start spending their money while others give to their parent to thank them for their support while they were jobless or saw them through college.

The scripture says that we should honor the Lord with the first fruit of all our increase. We are not to spend our first income because it is holy unto God. Our first salary or wage should be given wholly to God. You are not to remove tithe from it rather it should be given all as first fruit to God.

> *Ezekiel 44:30*
> *And the first of all the firstfruits*
> *of all things, of every*
> *oblation of all, of every sort*
> *of your oblations, shall be*
> *the priest's: ye shall also give*
> *unto the priest the first*
> *of your dough, that he may cause*
> *the blessing to rest in*
> *thine house. (KJV)*

When you collect your first wage, you should take it to church and give it as first fruit. Your first wage or salary belongs to God. You are not to tithe nor give an offering from it, but all should be given to God. Therefore, get an envelope and put all your first wage and write on it first fruit. If the amount is a lot, write a check of the complete amount. If there had been any deduction from your employer as we expect there should be, write the total amount of what is left and give it as first fruit unto God. When you do this, you have committed God to bless your job, career, or business and no devil will have access to attack you.

The reason why many experience stagnation in their job with years of service without promotion could be that their first wage was not given to God, so the blessing did not come upon their job. If you are experiencing an attack of the enemy in your job or business and you remember that you did not give your first wage as the first fruit to God, then go to him in prayers, ask for mercy and he will show you exactly what to do.

If you were working somewhere and you decided to change job or got an offer from another job which you accept, then your first wage in that new job must be given as first fruit to God. I know it is not easy to give your entire wage to God, but we as born-again Christians are obliged to give so that the blessing will come upon the works of our hands. I had refused to give my first fruits in the past and I lost jobs and, experienced stagnation and many other attacks from the enemy, and when I gave my first fruits, I know the blessings that I experienced.

If you open a shop or run your own business, your first profit in your business must be given to God as the first fruit if you want your business to succeed. If you are a farmer, your first harvested crops must be given to God as the first fruit. You may ask, how possible that I should harvest an entire field of crops and take it to church? Well, that is the word of God and if you are a child of God who is ready to obey the word of God, then why not try God by doing it and see if you will not end up as the breadwinner of your nation through that simple obedience. You may be surprised how God will increase your farm to the point that thousands of people will have to work for you. Obedience to scriptural instructions is our highway to greatness.

If they obey and serve him, they shall spend their days in prosperity, and their years in pleasure.
Job 36:11 (KJV)

If we obey God's word and do it, he says we shall spend our days in prosperity. If he says we should give our first fruit to him so that the blessings will come upon the work of our hands, we should obey and through that obedience, we will prosper every day in what we do, and every day will be a pleasure for us while others are complaining.

CHAPTER 12

TITHE AND SACRIFICE

Genesis 22:2
And he said, take now thy son, thine only son Isaac, whom thou lovest, and get thee into the land of Moriah; and offer him there for a burnt offering upon one of the mountains which I will tell thee of. (KJV)

The tithe is not a sacrifice and sacrifice is not tithe. Many Christians think that they can use the tithe to give as sacrifice thereby trying to force the hand of God to respond to their needs. They also think that paying tithes is a kind of sacrifice because according to them, paying tithes takes a lot from them. Tithe, as rightly defined, is the ten percent of our earnings. **Sacrifice on the other hand is giving something to God that cost us much thereby invoking the hand of God upon a specific situation in our life.** You are not making a sacrifice by paying your tithe because you don't make a sacrifice by paying your tax. If paying tax is a sacrifice, then we would be protesting in the streets. Sacrifice is not an obligation. We willingly sacrifice to secure a supernatural intervention.

> *2 Kings 3:26-27*
> *And when the king of Moab saw that the battle was too sore for him, he took with him seven hundred men that drew swords, to breakthrough even unto the king of Edom: but they could not.* ***Then he took his eldest son that should have reigned in his stead, and offered him for a burnt offering upon the wall.*** *And there was great indignation against Israel: and they departed from him, and returned to their own land. (KJV)*

Every time I read this passage in scripture, I always say to myself; "this is sacrifice indeed".

The above scripture gives us a vivid explanation of what sacrifice is. The king of Moab was in a terrible situation that seemed to have no way out, and after trying all that he could as a human, nothing seemed to work; he took his eldest son and offered him as a sacrifice and God stepped in and open a way for him. To sacrifice your son, I mean your eldest son who should take over from you in the event of your demise, is the greatest sacrifice a man could make.

As I said earlier, sacrifice is something that must cost us. If what you give as a sacrifice does not cost you then it is not a sacrifice. We notice that after the king sacrificed his own son, God started fighting for him and doors were open to him. If you are experiencing a situation in your life that you have tried everything humanly possible and it seemed not to work, try sacrificing something, and then you will see God respond promptly. You may ask, "do I have to make a sacrifice before God respond? You must understand one thing that the kingdom of darkness is out to contest every blessing of God in our life. But when you raised an altar of sacrifice, God will not keep quiet anymore and allow the devil to have his way but will step in promptly.

God responds to sacrifice. You don't have to be very rich before you sacrifice neither do I ask you to take your child and sacrifice to God. A sacrifice could be anything. There was a time I had nothing, and God ask me to give him a sacrifice. I looked around and saw that I had nothing then I went back to him and said I have nothing to give then he responded in Psalm 116:17,

I will offer to thee the sacrifice of thanksgiving, and will call upon the name of the Lord. (KJV)

God was at this time asking me to do something that will cost me my comfort and my sleep. To offer a sacrifice of thanksgiving, you must wake up at midnight and sing praises and give thanks to God despite the prevailing circumstance. That will not be a comfortable situation if you do it sacrificially. Sometimes you must praise and give thanks for hours in the night. If you sleep well and wake up in the morning and begin to sing praises, that is not a sacrifice of praise and thanksgiving.

At another time God asked me to give him a sacrifice, I looked around and the only thing I had was a laptop and it meant a lot to me. It was my most valuable possession. At that time, I couldn't do without that laptop and God said I should give that to him but after many attempts trying to run away from it, I finally gave him that laptop. I took it to church and put it in the offering basket and my destiny opened. When God asks you to give him a sacrifice, he will always put something in your heart. He told Abraham to sacrifice his only son. He didn't mention someone else but Isaac.

Your tithe can never be your sacrifice. Don't give your tithe and think that you are giving a sacrifice to God. Know that whenever God wants to change your level, he may prompt you in your heart to give something that will cost you just like he did with Abraham in order to establish His covenant with him forever. There are times you may not need to wait for God but decide to force him to respond to a situation. You can decide to give him something of value

WHY YOU SHOULD ~~NOT~~ PAY YOUR TITHE

and he will certainly show up. A sacrifice is a one-time thing while tithe is what we must do continually as long as we earn income.

CHAPTER 13

TITHE AND TAX

Mark 12:17
And Jesus answering said unto them, render to Caesar the things that are Caesar's, and to God the things that are God's. And they marvelled at him. (KJV)

The tithe is kingdom tax. Your tithe is the kingdom tax that you are obligated to pay. As a Christian, you are expected to pay your tax. There are many Christians who refuse to fulfill this obligation because they think that they are not supposed to pay their tax. You're being born again does not exempt you from obeying the law and doing your duties to your country. There are some religious groups who refuse to sing the national anthem of their country or where they reside, yet they make use of every benefit that country has to offer. This is preposterous. **You cannot live in a country, make use of all that country has to offer yet refuse to pay your tax or sing the national anthem** of that country. Singing the national anthem of the nation you live in is not a sin. When Jesus was confronted with the issue of tax, he quickly responded by paying. If Jesus whom you claim to follow paid tax, then you have no excuse under any religious guise or dogma than to pay.

Mathew 17:27
Notwithstanding, lest we should
offend them, go thou
to the sea, and cast an hook,
and take up the fish that
first cometh up; and when
thou has opened his mouth,
thou shall find a piece of
money: that take, and give unto
them for me and thee. (KJV)

The above scripture clearly explains that as followers of Jesus, we are not exempted from our constitutional duties. We have an obligation to our country as we do also have obligation to our home country- heaven.

As much as we pay our tax, we must pay our tithe. You can't be paying tax faithfully to avoid a problem with the government and refuse to pay tithe. Your tax is for your country and your tithe is for your home country. As born-again Christians, our real home is heaven. We are citizens of heaven resident on the earth. If you allow this understanding gets into you, you will mind every kingdom's demand.

Your tax is what the government uses in making things work, like building or repairing roads, giving you electricity and gas in your homes, making sure that water is available for your everyday use. The reason why you complain anytime you pass through a bad road or when electricity fails is because you are a taxpayer, and you expect the authorities to do something about it. Thus, your tithe is what is being used to make things work and move the kingdom of God on the earth. Your local church where you are to pay your tithe uses the tithes to pay their bills. If you don't pay your tithes, the work of God may not move forward.

I have heard many Christians say that they cannot be paying tax and pay their tithe at the same time. Know that you cannot do one and leave the other. Also, if you pay your tithe and refuse to pay your tax, God will not be happy with you because you are expected to obey the government.

Let every soul be subject unto the higher powers.
For there is no power but of God:
the powers that be are ordained of God.
Whosoever therefore resisteth the power,
resisteth the ordinance of
God: and they that resist shall receive
to themselves damnation.
For rulers are not terror to good works,
but to the evil. Will thou
then not be afraid of the power? ***Do that which is good****, and thou shalt have praise of the same.*
Romans 13:1-3

God asks us to submit to the authorities. If you refuse to obey the government by fulfilling your constitutional obligation, you are disobeying God.

Finally, you cannot obey the government and disobey God. You must do both. Pay your tithe, pay your tax.

CHAPTER 14

BENEFITS OF TITHING

Malachi 3:10-11
Bring ye all the tithes into the store-house, that there may be meat in mine house, and prove me now herewith, saith the LORD of hosts, if I will not open you the windows of heaven, **and pour you out a blessing, that there shall not be room enough to receive it. And I will rebuke the devourer for your sakes, and he shall not destroy the fruits of your ground; neither shall your vine cast her fruit before the time in the field,** *saith the LORD of hosts.*

There are many benefits accrued to tithers as outlined in the opening scripture and enjoyed by those who have engaged in this kingdom mystery. Before I became an addicted tither, I used to struggle with finances. I was also plagued with sicknesses. It seemed that the heavens over me were closed, and my business crumbled, I lost my fiancée and my life turned upside down. I did not think it had anything to do with tithe as I tried everything possible to get back at my feet. When the mystery of tithing was shown to me, I decided to engage in it with all my heart and today the difference is clear. I believe one of the reasons why you are reading this book today is because I am a tither. I don't struggle for anything, and no amount of money seems too much for me. I am not anxious about anything, and my life is peaceful.

God says that when you pay your tithe, He will rebuke the devourer for your sakes. Many negative things that happen in people's life are caused by the devourer. The devil is out to destroy mankind and worst if you identify with God by giving your life to Jesus. When you pay your tithe, it becomes the sole responsibility of the almighty God to rebuke the devil who is out to devour everything that concerns you.

TITHE BRINGS FINANCIAL BREAKTHROUGH

You cannot be a tither and live in penury. No tither goes around begging nor borrowing to live. When you pay your tithe, God causes your finances to be blessed. Any small business you do experiences breakthrough. While others are complaining that their weekly or monthly wages are not enough and start looking for a second or third job, you will be living well and in comfort. As a tither, anywhere you put your money will yield good returns. You cannot have a miscarriage in your business, and the devil will not have access to destroy the works of your hand. The reason why many put money into some business and lost it all is that they are not tithers. If you are a tither, God is committed to protecting your finances and the works of your hand.

TITHE BRINGS HEALING, HEALTH, AND WHOLENESS

Tithe can bring healing, health, and wholeness to you and your family. You cannot pay your tithes and be taken from one hospital to another in search of health. You cannot be a tither and be paying hospital bills. Either you are paying hospital bills, or you are paying your tithes. You cannot do both. Every sickness and disease in anyone's life, is a devourer at work, whether they are born again or not. Know that sickness or disease is a spirit, that is why God says he will rebuke the spirit who is causing that sickness for your sake.

The devil is a devourer, and he is a spirit and when you understand this you will know where afflictions come from. The greatest need of man is good health and many including wealthy men have spent a great amount of money looking for good health. I live in the United States of America and have seen billions of dollars being spent every year by people just to stay healthy. People are so mindful of which health insurance they have, and the insurance companies have milked the entire system because of health issues. Legislations and health policies are serious issues, and it concerns everybody. One can win a presidential election just by promising a better health care policy. You can live healthy without bothering about the cost of health insurance by being a tither. This may sound ridiculous to many, but the truth is that God's word is immutable. There are many people, me inclusive who live sickness-free by obeying God's word in Malachi 3:10.

TITHE TERMINATE CURSES.

Tithe can overwrite every negative pattern that was initiated in your lineage or blood line. There are many people who are living under generational curses or affliction. There are things that affect their lineage and have been passed down from one generation to another. These were either acquired ignorantly or intentionally by their forefathers or mothers through a covenant they entered with a spirit, or it could be an attack from the enemy of their family. These afflictions could be seen through hereditary diseases, bad luck, untimely death, or lack of breakthroughs. When you pay your tithe, these afflictions could be wiped off your lineage. You can be the reason why your family begins to enjoy a life free from curses by becoming a tither.

WHY YOU SHOULD ~~NOT~~ PAY YOUR TITHE

TITHE BRINGS PROMOTIONS AND DELIVERS FROM DESTRUCTION.

There is a brother who was delivered from armed robbers when they came to the apartment where he lived and robbed everyone. As they got close to his apartment, he removed his tithe booklet and put it by the door, and went back to sleep, the robbers did not come to his house but robbed others. I believe if he was not a tither, he would have been robbed. Tithes have delivered so many people from the devouring power of the devil and you too can be delivered if you engage in this mystery.

Tithe can stop miscarriage and make you deliver your child safely. There are some people who experience miscarriage every time they are pregnant; why not tithe and see that beautiful baby sustained in your womb to the shame of the enemy. You can open your destiny by tithing, you can walk under open heavens by tithings, and you can experience success in your exam by being a tither. As I said earlier, the devil is out to destroy, and he is an unrepentant destroyer. He does not have remorse nor will stop devouring. He has a threefold agenda **to**

steal, kill; and destroy and he will do just that till the end of time.

> *The thief cometh not, but for to steal,*
> *and to kill, and to destroy: I am come*
> *that they might have life, and that they*
> *might have it more abundantly.*
> *John 10:10 (KJV)*

The only way out is to engage in a mystery that will cause God who can stop him to respond on your behalf. That promotion you are looking for in your job or business is possible if you are a tither.

Tithe can save you from accidents and evil arrows. Anything that will devour your time, resources and family can be overcome through the mystery of tithing. It is important for us to know that God is faithful, and He will not go against His word. If He says devourer will be rebuked for your sake, that is certain. You don't have to disturb a pastor to pray for you or run around town seeking a solution when you can simply remain in the covenant.

WHY YOU SHOULD ~~NOT~~ PAY YOUR TITHE

As a tither, it doesn't matter who hates you, your tithe will always protect you and open doors for you. If you notice any negative trend in your life or family, start tithing or tithe faithfully and see that trend disappear. In my family, no one ever succeeds. They can try but eventually return to the floor. There are many drunkard uncles of mine who were once promising but the family challenge reduced them to nothing. Marriage in my family was not desirable. No one got married properly, they met and starts living together. I was the first to do an engagement, pay the traditional bride price, and do a white wedding. After me, doors open for others, my sister got married almost immediately to a man with two master's degrees whereas she has only a high school diploma. That is what tithe can do. A tither can never fail or be brought low in life. God's word is sure, and He will always remain faithful.

CHAPTER 15

WINDOWS OF HEAVEN

Malachi 3:10-11
*Bring ye all the tithes into the store-house, that there may be meat in mine house, and prove me now herewith, saith the LORD of hosts, **if I will not open you the windows of heaven**, and pour you out a blessing, that there shall not be room enough to receive it. (KJV)*

There is no other giving in the scripture that God promises to open the windows of heaven. When I first read this passage, I wondered what God mean by the 'windows of heaven. Many people including preachers of the word have interpreted this phrase as money and so many Christians pay

WHY YOU SHOULD ~~NOT~~ PAY YOUR TITHE

their tithes hoping that money will begin to come from everywhere and when it doesn't happen, they get frustrated and stop tithing.

The "windows of heaven" in this context mean divine ideas. You see God is not man and his ways can never be like our way. When you pay your tithe, God will respond by giving you an idea that if you run with it, will bring you enormous wealth. Everyone who pays their tithes genuinely has been given a rain of divine ideas but because they are looking for who will give them a check of a million dollars, they missed out on what could have changed their story forever. Most times those ideas could sound very stupid, and they just ignore it not knowing it is their highway to greatness.

There is a sister in my church who is a faithful tither and one day God drop an idea in her spirit, and she started hearing "water". Each time she prays she kept hearing the word "water" and so she began to sell water, today she has bottled water factories and she is living in wealth. It came as an idea. That is the blessing from the windows of heaven that was open to her. If you look at that scripture, it says "windows" which means many accesses to a divine idea. God can give you opportunities for creativity. This book you are reading is an idea from God. I don't look at what others wrote and decide to write. A topic will just drop in my spirit, and I begin to write. I have written so many books and all of them are different topics that I never thought about writing, they just drop in my spirit, and I write.

Therefore, as a tither, God will always drop in your spirit an idea that can change your status. In your career, God can show you what to do that will promote you and take you from the background to the management level. As a student, God can give you an idea that will make you an employer of labor so that you finish from high school or college living in wealth.

Don't pay your tithe and expect an increase in salary or wage or expect to win a lottery or someone just favors you with money. Listen to your spirit because God can give you an idea to do something and if you do it, the world will hear about you and celebrate you. Ideas rule the world and if God is to change your level, He will always give you a divine idea, that is the blessing from the windows of heaven.

CHAPTER 16

ANALYZING MALACHI 3:10-11

Bring ye all the tithes into the store-house, that there may be meat in mine house, and prove me now herewith, saith the LORD of hosts, if I will not open you the windows of heaven, and pour you out a blessing, that there shall not be room enough to receive it. And I will rebuke the devourer for your sakes, and he shall not destroy the fruits of your ground; neither shall your vine cast her fruit before the time in the field, saith the LORD of hosts. (KJV)

In this chapter, we will take an in-depth look at Malachi 3:10-11. Many of us have read, recite, and even preached on this verse of

WHY YOU SHOULD ~~NOT~~ PAY YOUR TITHE

the bible but may not really investigate it deeply. Many pastors have used this verse to coerce their members into submission to bring their tithes, but they do not understand fully what it means except to bring in tithes.

The verse starts by saying "bring all the tithes." What does this mean? The scripture says bring in all the tithe, not some. You see, bringing in all the tithes applies both to the giver and the receiver. It is an error to think that only the church member should bring in all the tithe and the pastor can have money without giving it all back to God. When the tithes come in from members, the pastor must ensure that the church tithes from that tithe including all other finances from non-tithe giving. It's a two-way thing, the members bring, and you too bring.

Members should ensure that the tithe they are giving is the complete tithe not partial. You cannot divide your tithe and pay half this month saying that you will complete the other half next month. That is wrong. Don't keep back the tithe, don't pay some, and don't calculate wrong tithe and pay. It is better for God to cheat you by you paying more than for you to cheat God. **When you cheat God, is robbery but when God cheats you, is a blessing.**

The scripture also says, "into the storehouse." The storehouse here implies your place of worship. Don't take your tithe to where you are not fed spiritually. Heaven will only receive tithe given in the storehouse. You must be born again and belong to a particular place of worship before the tithe is acceptable. Traveling around to pay your tithe is not tithe paying but philanthropy. You must bring the tithe into the storehouse so "that there may be meat in mine house." Here God is saying that when you bring your tithe to your place of worship called storehouse, your tithe will provide for that storehouse, it will make things available for God's work in that church.

God also says, "prove me now herewith, saith the LORD of hosts." God here is giving an open invitation to tithers to "test" him. He says you should try and see. You know when a deity dares you, it means he is serious and ready. You can't try God and He fails you. He asks us to try and see "if I will not open you the windows of heaven, and pour you out a blessing, that there shall not be room enough to receive it." The windows here mean divine ideas.

You see, people pay tithes and expect that money will just pour from heaven for them. Some expect that they would wake up and see money under their pillow or they will win a lottery. They are just dreaming because that is not how God works. He says he will open the windows and pour out a blessing. Look at this deeply. How can windows be open and only a blessing is poured out? Windows supposed to bring blessings instead He says a blessing. That is one blessing. God will only give you an idea that can bring you great wealth if you pay attention. You don't need lots of ideas to make it, just one. Sometimes the idea may not make sense but if it comes from God and you run with it, the sky will only be the beginning.

Remember God says, "you will not have room enough to receive it." This means that if you engage in tithing, I will give you an idea that your capacity may not be able to carry. Some pastors preach this to mean that you will have so much wealth that you will not have space to keep them. This could be true in a literal sense but on the flip side, you should build capacity to be able to manage the blessing. While you tithe, build capacity. Get an education, build meaningful relationships that can help you manage the blessing. Don't be a tither and sit down. When God opens heaven over you through divine ideas, you may crash if you don't know how to handle it. If it means you go back to school or get a higher education, it will certainly help you. Managing resources is very important and the earlier you build capacity the better. Not having room enough does not mean that money will come, and the banks may not be able to keep it, no it means ability, or intellectual capacity to maintain it.

Another important thing that God says here is, "and I will rebuke the devourer for your sakes, and he shall not destroy the fruits of your ground." There are devourers whether you believe it or not. Tithe gives God the responsibility of securing your wealth and life. It is true that you can succeed in life by becoming wealthy without God, but that success or wealth is not secure. I have seen

WHY YOU SHOULD ~~NOT~~ PAY YOUR TITHE

many people who were very successful, they had everything going for them but one day the wealth and success vanished. I believe you have seen or heard such.

The tithe is security. God says He will rebuke the devourer. The devourer here is the devil and his primary assignment is to steal, kill and destroy John 10:10. If you want to secure your life and property, engage in the mystery of tithing. If God rebukes the devourer, he will not touch you, your business, or your family. Everyone wants to live a secure life and the surest way to do that I believe is the tithe.

The tithe verses conclude by saying "he shall not destroy the fruits of your ground; neither shall your vine cast her fruit before the time in the field." God himself says that He will not allow the devil to destroy the fruit of your ground. The fruit of your ground here is your business or job. He will not allow you to be sacked from a job that is providing for your family. If by any chance that happens, a better job will come your way with bigger pay. If you are a tither and you lose your job, relax a better job is coming soon.

As a self-employ, the fruit of your ground is your business and God will not allow the devil to destroy it. You will not lose a contract or open a shop, and no one is buying. In fact, no matter what you do or sell, tithe makes you excel. God can bless any business it doesn't matter the size or location. You will not also cast your young before the time. Here God is saying that you will not have a premature delivery, and nothing will die in your hand. This is amazing because the devil wants to see you fail. He wants to see you miscarry. But God will keep you from a negative experience in your business or carrier. Your wife will not get pregnant and miscarry, and you will not be among those to be downsized in your job. You will start a business and succeed. The divine idea will become fruitful and make you a generational blessing.

CHAPTER 17

HOW TO ENFORCE ANSWERS TO DELAYED RETURNS

Isaiah 43:26
Put me in remembrance: let us plead together:
declare thou, that thou mayest be justified. (KJV)

Some tithers do not have returns for their tithing.

There was a time when my phone fell, and I took it to the repairer and spent about a hundred and forty dollars to repair. I was angry in my spirit because as a tither I should not be spending money repairing my phone. That was a devourer. Just few days later, the phone fell again and the screen damaged, I was so upset that I told God this is unacceptable. I cannot pay tithe and He allow the devourer to have a access in my life. I demanded that this should stop and that I am not going to spend a dime repairing the phone and would not stay without a phone. I did what the above scripture says, I declared, and I was justified. A word came to my spirit that I should take it back to the person who repaired it and when I got there, he just collected the phone and fixed it without charging me any money. And since then, the phone has been working well even though it has fallen many times.

You can demand answers to delayed returns. As a tither, you are expected to have returns from your tithe. When you pay your tax, you expect the government to fix the road and provide basic amenities for your comfort and if they don't, you demand to know why. You have the right to demand for any delayed returns from tithe. If you notice that things are not going on well in your life, business, academics, or career, you must demand answers. God says you should put him in remembrance of his word. Does it mean that God forget, no. God remembers and know everything, but He wants us to seek him. You see, God wants us to be closer to Him in fellowship than just doing things for us. If you have a healthy relationship with God, you may not need to pray for anything because there are those who before they ask, God respond.

In my case, If I kept quiet, I would be spending money repairing my phone when I have total coverage because of tithing. If you are experiencing stagnation in your business, demand to know why by going to God. The devil is out to contest our breakthrough that is why tithe is the only thing that can commit God to act on our behalf. Every other giving will bring returns, but tithe is the only giving that guarantees security. But if you are not getting anything back, demand answers.

I know of a single mother whose son had applied for jobs and each time he was denied. One day, as he was preparing to go for another job interview, the mother took the bible and open to Malachi 3:10 and began to pray. She told God that if His word is true as it is written, the son should not fail that interview. The son went and passed the interview and got the job. If you experience lack of returns for your tithing and things are happening to you as if you are a non-tither, go to God using his word as it is written. He says you should keep reminding him of his word. When the devil contends with you, remind God that he must rebuke him for your sake.

Don't keep writing one exam too many times, let your tithe speak for you. You can't be having miscarriages as a tither; your business cannot close when you are a tither. Whatever negative experiences you may have, hold God by his word and invoke Him to act on your behalf. That brother put his tithe booklet at the door of his house and armed robbers could not rob him, what he did was to enforce answer to returns for his tithes. He knew what to do and was delivered. Any blessing that has been delayed can be forced down through putting God to remembrance of His word.

Your tithe can bring you favor. If as a lady, no man has come to seek your hand in marriage when you are eligible, go to God and ask why.

But I must warn you when you stand before God let your hands be clean. Let's not take spiritual things for granted. It is not enough to tithe and continue to live in sin. If you are clean, you can lift your face unto God, and He will answer. You cannot be a faithful tither and have boyfriend on the side and expect God to touch his heart to marry you. Your tithe will not answer for you.

Many people tithe and expect answers but the reason why it has not happened is because they are living in sin. These same people now discourage others from paying tithe. Sin is a sinker even with your consistent tithing. There was a time in my life that I was not pleasing God with my life. One day, I took a lot of tithes to church and my conscience began to torment me. It said to me, if you can put your life in order, it would be better for you than giving in church. I gave the money that day, but I knew in my spirit that it was a waste.

God wants us more than our giving. He will bless us if only we surrender fully to Him. It does not take anything for God to transform our lives, but the limitation is in the way we live. I would rather tell you to settle with God first than to give. If your life is not right, stop giving and straighten out with God first. I know some pastors will not like what I am saying because they are more interested in the money but that is the truth. Settle your spiritual life first before you continue in your giving, so that it can go up to God as a "sweetsmelling savour."

The reason why many run all over the place trying to do something for God to bless them is because they have not fully surrender to Him. **Try and live a clean life, and you will pray less**. Prayer would only be a means of communicating with the father and not asking for bread and butter. It is good to tithe but it must go alongside righteousness. You would not need to bombard heaven for answer to delayed returns from your tithe if you are living right, things will just fall in place for you. Isaiah 65:24 says, *"and it shall come to pass, that before they call, I will answer; and while they are yet speaking, I will hear."* God is saying here that before you call, He will answer. To enter this dimension of life is to live clean. Stay away from sin, live a holy life and your tithe will enforce answer for you without you demanding for it. Tithe is not a substitute for Holiness.

Finally, be aware that whatever you do affect generations unborn. If you pay your tithe, your unborn children and grandchildren also pay tithe through you. Giving to a deity brings serious consequence on your family. The reason why many African and South American people suffer and live in abject poverty despite abundant natural resource is because of this issue. Their forefathers had covenants with marine spirits and sorcerers. They sacrificed to the gods and made pact with evil spirits not knowing that the consequence would be upon generations unborn. If you invest in the true God, your generations will be blessed.

Tithe can eradicate evil from your bloodline. God says you should do it and try Him if He will not rebuke devourer for your sake. If your family has been experiencing untimely death, marital delay, miscarriages, failure at the edge of breakthrough, sickness, and all manner of evil; these are devourers and only God can rebuke theme through your tithe. If there is a door you have been trying to open and it seems impossible, remind God of His word and He will open it easily for you. Do not allow the devil to keep you down. Anything that is not consistent with the word of God in your life, take it back to Him in prayer and he will answer you.

CHAPTER 18

DO NOT ROB GOD

Malachi 3:8
Will a man rob God? Yet ye have robbed me.
But ye say, Wherein have we robbed thee?
In tithes and offerings. (KJV)

Not paying your tithe is robbing God.

The tithe belongs to God and must be remitted. When you refuse to pay your tithe or use it for other purposes, you are a robber or thief before God. You cannot rob a deity and go free; it is not possible. When I was growing up, I used to see children enter a shrine and take things like food kept for the gods and eat. They did that when the priest of that shrine was not available. Fear did not allow me to join

WHY YOU SHOULD ~~NOT~~ PAY YOUR TITHE

them because I believed in my little mind that the spirits in the shrine will punish them. I was right as some of them died young or lived frustrated lives. But know that the consequences of such action only affect non-believers. The point is that there are consequences when you rob a deity.

The lives of believers who are non-tither can be clearly distinguished from those who tithe. Surrendering your tithe to God brings Him into your affairs. He takes control of your life, career, and business but if you don't tithe, He stays away. God takes tithe seriously and calls those who don't pay, robbers. This is scary when the supreme commander of the universe says you robbed Him. It is better to live with limited resources than to rob God of His share. When I did not pay my tithes for sometimes, I was still spending on food and clothes, and my conscience kept blaming me. One day, it said to me that God has been keeping me at my job, protecting me, and did not allow any evil to come to me, why do you refuse to give Him the little that belongs to Him. My heart broke, I lost interest in everything. I promised myself that I will start to pay my tithe consistently. You cannot take from a deity and be restful. Using the tithe to balance rent, buy food for the family or buy a gift for the pastor will only get us into trouble. God wants us to separate His tithe from what He gave to us.

Robbing God is taking His own and thinking that it does not matter. Many believers are robbers waiting for judgment, and when it comes, they run around looking for pastors to pray and cancel. I pray that pastors should begin to seek for the gift of discernment to know the source of the problem anytime members run to them. This will help them to pray less.

Many things plaquing believers are because of their non-tithing habit. Many will live in divine health if only they pay their tithe. God always has a way of getting His portion back. If you rob God by not paying your tithe, you may start paying hospital bills, be affected by a natural disaster, accidents, or failures that will cost you. It is better to pay than to spend the money on terrible situations and circumstances. A simple pull-over by the police could be because of you not paying your tithe.

WHY YOU SHOULD ~~NOT~~ PAY YOUR TITHE

Sometimes they can give you a ticket that is ridiculous and you ask yourself why me. Do not rob God, give Him His portion and you will live a restful life.

CHAPTER 19

DYNAMICS OF GOD'S KINGDOM FINANCES

Haggai 2:8
The silver is mine, and the gold is
mine, saith the LORD of hosts. (KJV)

There are ways money work in the kingdom.

God is the owner of everything. He says the silver and the gold belong to him. I believe God will never lay claim to what is not His. It will be a dent of character to his person if he says that the silver and gold belong to him when it does not. For God to say that money belongs to him, then it means he is the originator of wealth. In Psalm 24:1, God lay claims to the whole world.

> *The earth is the Lord's and the fulness thereof;*
> *the world, and they that dwell therein.*
> *Also, in 1Corinthians 10:26*
> *For the earth is the Lord's,*
> *and the fulness thereof. (KJV)*

Both the old and the New Testament confirms that God is the owner of the whole earth, including everything in it, that is why He is called LORD. Since God is the owner of everything, that means he is the custodian of wealth. Now that we understand this, we should know that there is a way money works in the kingdom. God is a God of order and principle and because he is faithful, he can never go against the principle that he set in motion. For you to prosper in God's kingdom, you must understand how it works.

Many Christians think that they can force the hand of God to prosper them financially through fasting and prayer. If you like, call all the men of God to come and pray, prophecy and even pour all the anointing oil on your piece of land, it will never produce anything until you sow a seed on that land. When you sow, you don't need any prayer or fasting for your seed to grow. Prayer and fasting are good because it empowers us and keep the devil at a distance so we can dominate effortlessly but if you want money, you will have to sow. I have never seen anyone who holds a key to the door but decides to pray for the door to open. The key to financial prosperity is seedtime and harvest and when you have this key, you begin to live in financial abundance.

The tithe is the key that unlocks supernatural wealth. The reason why the tithe is the master key to financial prosperity is that among other giving in the scripture, it is only tithe that opens the windows of heaven and rebukes the devourer. All other giving will bring returns because the word of God is true as recorded in Luke 6:38

WHY YOU SHOULD ~~NOT~~ PAY YOUR TITHE

Give, and it shall be given unto you; good measure, pressed down, and shaken together, and running over, shall men give into your bosom. For with the same measure that ye mete withal it shall be measured to you again. (KJV)

But when you tithe, something supernatural begins to happen in your life. Not only will you have returns, but you also begin to walk under an open heaven and any devourer sent your way becomes the sole responsibility of the Almighty God to rebuke.

There are many believers who are givers, not tithers and they are blessed through their giving, but there is no security to their wealth. When God blesses you, the enemy is angry at your blessing and wants to contest it. This he does through attacking your health, and when your health is attacked, it means your finance is under attack because it is your finance that you will use to look for good health. The enemy can also attack your family, your peace, and even the works of your hand. When you tithe, the enemy cannot attack you because the seal of absolute protection against such attack has been set in motion.

The way money works in the kingdom of God is not the same way it works in the world. The world believes that hard work and luck make rich but in the kingdom of God, giving is what brings wealth. The bible says in Proverb 11:24

> *Those who give generously receive more,*
> *but those who are stingy with what*
> *is appropriate will grow needy. (CEB)*

In the kingdom of God, giving is what brings more and failure to give only leads to poverty. But you may ask what about those who don't serve or give to God but keep getting richer? My answer is in Psalm 73:7 and 17

> *Their eyes stand out with fatness: they*
> *have more than heart could wish.....*
> *Until I went into the sanctuary of God;*
> *then understood I their end. (KJV)*

You see, those who do not give to God but accumulate for themselves always have a

WHY YOU SHOULD ~~NOT~~ PAY YOUR TITHE

terrible end. Do you remember the rich fool in the bible who ignored God? we all know how he ended, Luke 12:20. Giving is living and when you serve God with your resources, you will live well here on earth and in heaven.

People in the world bribe their way through, but for you as a believer, tithe can open doors for you. You do not need to soil a hand to breakthrough, simply tithe. Many women in business and career believe that the only way to the top is to sleep with a man but they failed to understand that when you sleep with someone to open a door for you, you will need to continue sleeping with them for that door to remain open. This is the way of the world but with God, all you need to do is give. When your tithe opens a door for you no human or spirit can close it.

The world also believes that for you to rise in life, you must bring somebody down, that is not so in the kingdom. We have seen this world's method of *making it* cause so many atrocities, people kill one another to make money, rob, lie, cheat, and even sell their bodies for money. But you do not need to stress yourself like that to *make it*, just obey and give and doors will be open to you. You don't need to kill or bring someone down for you to rise, you give your way to breakthrough. You can rise by raising someone up, that is the way of the kingdom of God.

The reason many fast and pray to become wealthy is because they do not want to submit to the scriptural demand of tithing. Fasting and prayer will never make you rich but covenant practice. Getting a headache and going for tuberculosis medication is foolishness. Instead of fasting and praying or running around looking for pastors to pray for your business to succeed, why not simply pay your tithe and see if your financial troubles will not be over.

God's ways are not our ways, prosperity in the kingdom of God is based on principle or keys and the application of these keys will bring wealth effortlessly. When you give, you increase, but when you accumulate for a selfish reason, you tend to poverty. In the kingdom of God, there is nothing like *getting rich quickly*. Giving, patience, hard work, and wisdom bring wealth.

WHY YOU SHOULD ~~NOT~~ PAY YOUR TITHE

God needs people to help advance His purposes on the earth and He is ready to bless them just to do that. But if God must bless you financially, holiness is a must. Engaging in the covenant does not exempt you from living a righteous life. Bitterness, hatred, malice, grudges, envy, and evil speaking are spiritual blockades to kingdom wealth. Being a faithful tither will not make you prosperous if you engage in any of these sins. Avoid them at all costs, learn to forgive so that your channel of blessing can be clear and free to receive from the Father light.

Sin blocks prayers and makes total nonsense of your fasting. It brings dark clouds over your head and so the heavens cannot pour out for you. Learn to forgive people even before they offend you. Free those who hurt you from your heart no matter the degree of offense and you will be amazed at what your giving will procure for you. If you have offended somebody or know that someone is not happy with you because of an issue, reach out to them. Be the first to apologize and reconcile and doors that were blocked will begin to open to you. I am telling you what I did for my heavens to open. There are ways things work in the kingdom, giving alone will not make you prosperous if you have things standing against you in the spirit realm.

It is easier to make it in life with God than to follow the world's pattern. When God blesses you, it comes with peace and joy. When you make it the world's way, fear and sleeplessness become your partner. There is no armed robber who doesn't look over his shoulder or a murderer who sleeps well at night; if you find any please let me know. God's kingdom wealth carries peace along with it, seek for that.

It is important to understand that wealth in the kingdom is not for personal consumption. If all you want is for God to bless you financially so that you and your family can have a good life without kingdom mindset, then forget about God and look elsewhere. God will always put in your hand when you have His interest at heart. Kingdom wealth is to advance the kingdom. God will make you wealthy if you will be a kingdom financier. That is how it works. Let me ask you, how many church project have you funded? What type of secret investment have you made to advance the purposes of God without anyone knowing about it. I don't mean standing up in the church to pledge so that others will see and glorify you.

You see, if you want God to bless you lavishly, do things for Him that nobody knows about. Take up a project in your church or find something that is lacking in your church and provide according to your ability. I personally hate it when the church must budget for everything when there are members who can simply fill that need. Your church doesn't need to make announcement that there is a need when you are there. You don't need to be rich to make it happen, start from where you are. God is looking for people to showcase His end-time wealth, but you must have a track record before you can be that vessel. No one rises by mistake. Many people have done some crazy things behind the scene and when God raises them up, you begin to claim their blessing without any track record.

Look around your church to see if there is something you can do, then do it secretly and

God will reward you openly. Have a kingdom mindset, think of what you can do for God. If there is nothing for you to do, look at the church members, if there are committed members who wears same cloth all the time, buy new ones for them instead of gossiping. Whatever you do for others, you are doing it for God, Mathew 25:40.

Apart from giving to the church, learn to give to your pastors. As you are reading this, ask yourself if you have ever given anything to your pastor. Giving to your pastor is very important because it brings blessing to you and your family. The bible says in Proverb 11:25 *"The generous man [is a source of blessing and] shall be prosperous and enriched, And he who waters will himself be watered [reaping the generosity he has sown]."* (AMP) When you are generous with your pastor, God will make people generous to you. That is how it works. Don't go to church all the time, hear the preaching that the pastor spends time preparing, and leave without sowing seed. Your offering and tithe are not enough if you have never given anything to the person that prays for you and releases the blessing upon your life.

WHY YOU SHOULD ~~NOT~~ PAY YOUR TITHE

Sometimes, reach out to your pastor and sow seed no matter how small and God will bless you. During the festive season, buy your pastor a gift. Let me tell you the truth, a pastor will never come and tell you about his challenges, they learned to suffer in silence. A pastor may be preaching a hot sermon yet has no food at home. I learned this when I was a young boy. My mother bought foodstuff for our pastor at the time and send me to deliver; the pastor broke down in tears and wondered how my mother knew that they did not have anything to eat at home. I learned that day the importance of giving to pastors. The pastors who suffer most are those under a general overseer. People rarely give to them but when they hear that the general overseer will be coming, they package heavy seed to give whereas the pastor whom they see every day, never received anything. That is wickedness. The blessing you expect will not come if you neglect your pastor and give to another. Charity begins at home. Give to your pastor that you see always, and God will bless you. Buy things for your pastor and his family. When you provide for your pastor, the anointing will flow more, and he will continue to serve with joy.

Now that we learn about giving to the men and women of God that serve us, the pastors need to reciprocate by giving back. You may ask, should a pastor give back to members? Oh yes, he should. To be blessed, a pastor should give back to members. Preaching and praying for members is not enough. A pastor should go the extra mile to give back to members of his church and community.

As a pastor, find out the issues and challenges that confront your church members and see how you can help. The members give you money and material gifts but what they need may not be cash or material. For those living in the United States and the United Kingdom, the most pressing need is a *green card* or *papers*. Find out the need of members, seek information and or solution from different sources, and relate to your members. Learn to know about what is happening in your community and inform your members.

WHY YOU SHOULD ~~NOT~~ PAY YOUR TITHE

The church is not only for preaching and blessing but also for information that can help members. Some people come to church with a heavy burden. Sometimes it can be family challenges that preaching alone may not solve. Reach out and ask questions and you will be amazed. Bishop Oyedepo was preaching one day and noticed a man who was not smiling throughout the service. When he finished, he called for the man to ask what challenges he was facing only to find out that the man had nothing to feed his family with. The bishop gave the man all the offering of that Sunday service. You see, this is a pastor that understands that people come to church with different needs. If you think the only need of your church members is spiritual, then you are wrong. Giving back to your members like Bishop Oyedepo will make your church members bless you more in return.

CHAPTER 20

WHAT GAMBLERS SHOULD KNOW

> *Psalm 22:18*
> *They divide my clothes among them*
> *and cast lots for my garment. (NIV)*

> *Mathew 27:35*
> *When they had crucified him, they*
> *divided up his clothes by casting lots. (NIV*

Gambling is evil and does not glorify God.

The soldiers that crucified Jesus gambled for his clothes. They decided to throw a disc to win his clothes. Imagine killing a man and right there, gamble for his belonging, this is evil. There is nothing a gambler would not do. They can sell their properties to bet.

We have seen the rise in gambling through online betting and other sorts, this is the devil's way of destroying lives and destinies. Gambling is a cankerworm that has eaten deep into the very fabric of our society, no country is exempted. Unless God reveals to you in a dream or vision to bet, a Christian should never be involved. Those who win the lottery in millions of dollars never stay rich. I have not seen any prominent business where the owner made it through gambling. Instead, hard work, skill, and wisdom always grow and sustain a business. Prominent brands and lasting enterprises came through visions that were pursued.

It is important for gamblers to know that gambling is very addictive and can destroy your life just like hard drugs and alcohol. The little money you have if invested productively can yield great dividends. Spending time on betting boards and rolling discs in the casino can ruin your life just as it has ruined many.

What draws people to gambling is evil desire just like stealing. They don't want to work but want fast money. They want the good things of life without having to sweat for it and so they use the money they have to gamble for bigger money. James 1:14 says *"but each person is tempted when they are dragged away by their own evil desire and enticed."* The enticement to win more money and become rich quickly is what draws people to gambling and in the end, they lose everything. I have heard of casinos who make sure that if you win big money, they will do everything to keep you playing till you lose all. What is the benefit of that? Instead, why not stay in God, pay your tithe, give to advance His kingdom and He will decorate your life with dignity.

To gamble, you are neglecting God and giving your life over to luck. God does not make people lucky; it is the devil's trick of giving you something that will surely vanish. God grants favor and favor is what you need in life. Hard work is important as a believer, don't look for the shortest way to make it in life by giving yourself to gambling. Instead of gambling, pay

WHY YOU SHOULD ~~NOT~~ PAY YOUR TITHE

your tithe. Use the money that you would have used to place a bet at the casino to pay your tithe. Give it to a deity that will open the windows of heaven over you and stop evil from happening to you. We live in a dangerous time and the devil, and his agents are bent on destruction. Giving God part of your finance is inviting Him into your life and affair and when God takes over, no demon in hell can stop you.

Gambling makes you lose time and money, it results in frustration, suicide, and a ruined life. Growing up, I saw some men who used their salaries to play pool (a kind of Bet in my country). Many of them lost their families, job, friends and end up dead. Remember the devil does not love anyone and whatever he makes you do is to destroy you. The soldiers who gamble for Jesus' clothing did not become rich by it so the small money you win will certainly fly away. Gambling makes you live a life of covetousness, immorality, and drunkenness. You can overcome these by surrendering to Jesus and start using your money to promote the kingdom of God through giving and you will see how God will bless you beyond measure.

If you have been addicted to gambling and want to be helped, the first thing is to surrender your life to Jesus, accept him as your Lord and savior and he only can save you. When you become a child of God, you begin to pay your tithe in the church that you are a member of, and God will then bless whatever you do.

Finally, don't gamble, don't play pool, or do online betting. Do not play jackpot or mega millions. Be wise to understand that no one loves you and wants to give you millions of dollars free. The winners of a lottery never stay rich. They quickly spend the money and return to living in debt. God does not want you to gamble but to work with your hands and provide for yourself and be a blessing to others. Ephesians 4:28 *"Anyone who has been stealing must steal no longer, but must work, **doing something useful with their own hands**, that they may have something to share with those in need."* Do something with your hands, not gambling, get a job, or start a business. Don't sit around in pool houses or in casinos betting

WHY YOU SHOULD ~~NOT~~ PAY YOUR TITHE

away your money. Stop spending money buying lottery or jackpots and scratching away your destiny. Lean on God for supply and use the little you have to advance the kingdom and the blessing of heaven will be upon you and your entire household. God bless you richly.

EPILOGUE

Now that we have learned about tithe, I believe our understanding has been enlightened. The time has come to maximize this kingdom mystery to our benefit. It is important to obey God and be committed to His demands than to ignore them. God is committed to blessing us if we obey Him. *"For this is the love of God, that we keep his commandments: and his commandments are not grievous."* 1 John 5:3. The commandments of God are not grievous but an express road to our blessings. Our commitment to obeying God attracts Him into our lives. Obedience is the key that unlocks supernatural favor and divine supply. The tithe is a key that can unlock supernatural blessing if we engage committedly.

WHY YOU SHOULD ~~NOT~~ PAY YOUR TITHE

Understand that no one become wealthy with a *clear eye*. Prosperity is a spiritual thing; you cannot wake up one day and become prosperous. Everybody does something behind the scenes to become wealthy. You need spiritual backup to become prosperous according to Deuteronomy 8:18 and Isaiah 48:17. A spirit must help you to *make it in life*, but you have the will to choose which one you need the help from. When you pay your tithe, you have chosen God as the Spirit you need help from, and He will not only help but also protect your wealth.

The blessing and protection that comes with tithing cannot be compared to other kingdom commitments. When we engage the mystery of tithing, we will open our lives to an unlimited flow of heavenly provision. Make tithing a kingdom habit, be committed and do it joyfully. I know it is not easy to comply with every kingdom demand but remember what Jesus says in Mathew 7:14, *"because strait is the gate, and narrow is the way, which leadeth unto life, and few there be that find it."* Serving God puts us in a narrow path, and that is the reason many do not want to serve. Many Christians wants to be comfortable; they want to serve God the way they want but it is not so in the kingdom. Our path as born again Christians is straight and narrow and when we follow this path, it leads to a fulfilled life here on earth and eternity in heaven. As you make up your mind to be a committed tither, God will continue to be committed to your affairs. Your time for a change of story has come. REMAIN EVER BLESSED.

All scriptures used are quoted in their respective translations and referred.

All sources duly cited.

If you have been blessed, impacted, or given your life to Jesus through reading this book, please reach out through the following:

Email: victoransor@yahoo.com

website: victoransor.com

Or write to us at:

VICTOR ANSOR PUBLISHING

22901 Linden Blvd

PO Box 110423

Cambria Heights NY 11411

GOD BLESS YOU